The Fairbanks Album

The Fairbanks Album

DRAWN FROM THE FAMILY ARCHIVES BY Douglas Fairbanks, Jr.

INTRODUCTION AND NARRATIVE BY Richard Schickel

NEW YORK GRAPHIC SOCIETY BOSTON

Library of Congress Cataloging in Publication Data
Main entry under title:

The Fairbanks album.

1. Fairbanks, Douglas, 1909- —Portraits, etc.
2. Fairbanks, Douglas, 1883-1939—Portraits, etc.
I. Fairbanks, Douglas, 1909- II. Schickel, Richard.
PN2287.F32F3 791.43'028'0922 75-9095
ISBN 0-8212-0637-0

Designed by Janet Halverson

First Edition

New York Graphic Society books are published by Little, Brown and Company.
Published simultaneously in Canada by Little, Brown and Company (Canada) Limited.

Printed in the United States of America

CONTENTS

FOREWORD BY DOUGLAS FAIRBANKS, JR. 7

INTRODUCTION 11

A Star is Born 27

The Modern Musketeer 45

Doug and Mary 79

Jayar and Pete 159

His Own Man 233

CHRONOLOGIES 281

PICTURE CREDITS 287

FOREWORD by Douglas Fairbanks, Jr.

THIS BOOK OWES ITS EXISTENCE to a strong streak of squirrelism that runs through my family. None of us seem able to throw anything away. So in all our attics and basements we are always rediscovering exotic shoehorns, broken umbrellas, boxes of paper clips, rusty music-boxes, files of ancient and trivial correspondence, crumbling receipts, scattered piles of long-forgotten snapshots, crates of albums. Even our old coat pockets surprise us with interesting finds, generally quite useless, sometimes unidentifiable or downright repulsive.

After considerable urging from my wife, friends, and secretary, who lack the hoarding gene, I agreed to a semi-ruthless weeding out of my own clutter. I parted reluctantly with even the most obviously useless scrap, but eventually the pyramids of paper and junk were reduced to a mere few thousand items. Over a period of a year or so these were catalogued and annotated, and huge albums were professionally prepared to preserve the most interesting.

But to whom they would eventually prove "most interesting" was uncertain, because neither my children nor my closest friends are as enthusiastic about our family's memorabilia as I insist on thinking they ought to be. Outsiders, on the other hand, had often encouraged me to think that some researcher in a forthcoming century might find in my collections just what he's looking for. I preferred their view, but made no decision about the final disposition of the material and just kept stashing away the newest generation of odds and ends, which began to accumulate immediately after my great clean-out.

In years past I had rather loftily declined proposals to "authorize" the publication of photographic biographies of my father and/or myself of the kind that in recent years has evidently found a ready market among the more fervently nostalgic. It wasn't long, however, before I found that the high-horse I'd been riding was a bucking bronco—for I learned, with honest surprise, that neither my authorization nor co-operation was in fact needed at all. Any publisher could, I was told, cull enough material from public sources to whip up a routine picture-book without so much as a by-your-leave from subject or heirs. Indeed, I learned that at least two publishing houses were mulling over plans for a Fairbanks family picture book.

Most of my family felt there was already enough on the Fairbankses "for the record": two fine biographies of my father, the first by my cousin, Letitia Fairbanks (in collaboration with Ralph

Hancock), called *The Fourth Musketeer,* and the other by Richard Schickel, *His Picture in the Papers.* There was also an excellent book about me by Brian Connell, *Knight Errant.* Still, the threat of a carelessly prepared book was beginning to give us second thoughts about closing the official—if that word isn't too pompous—record.

At about this time I was contacted by the New York Graphic Society, which proposed a family album drawing upon all pictorial sources—public and private—for what was hoped would prove a substantial history of my father's career and mine. When the publishers told me that Richard Schickel was willing to write the introduction and narrative as well as supervise the selection and grouping of the pictures, I was delighted, since I had admired his little book about my father and had come to know and trust him—as much as an actor ever trusts a critic.

I freely agreed to co-operate with author and publishers as much as possible, allowing them to browse to their hearts' content through the hoards of photographs, correspondence, clippings, and so forth that had been assembled on both sides of the Atlantic. In addition, I prevailed upon my cherished and always indulgent stepmother, Mary Pickford Rogers, to permit them to rummage through the scrapbooks at Pickfair, where she still lives with that wonderfully warm man, Buddy Rogers, whom she married after she and my father were divorced. And I turned to other relatives for even more tribal memorabilia. To them all, on behalf of them all, my thanks for their help and interest (and the publishers' as well).

Publishers and author thanked me heartily for the literally thousands of items submitted, and then added—with a certain embarrassment—that they could use only three or four hundred at most! The material selected could give only a general impression of highlights in the lives and careers of a father and son. I regret certain omissions, but this regret is tempered by the feeling that the story is sharpened by the limitations of creating a book of this kind, and that the resulting book will all the more likely answer my own strong desire that it should be as objective, as honest, as possible. Quite deliberately I have limited my role to the one defined on the jacket and title page. I did indeed draw, or cause to have drawn, material from the family archives. My principal contribution thereafter was to help reduce a mountain of documenta to a good-sized hill from which the author and editors made their decisions, to answer their questions, and to help identify places and people, especially some of those hauntingly familiar faces that keep appearing.

Most of my adult life I have tried to follow a bit of second-hand advice given me by my father on the opening night of *Young Woodley* in 1927, my first big part in the theater. He presented me with a bound copy of Sir Henry Irving's *The Art of Acting,* in which he had inscribed Hamlet's advice to the players: "Let your own discretion be your tutor." Keeping that maxim well in mind, I have, in regard to this book, assiduously avoided looking over the shoulder of an author I respect, and at this writing I have seen scarcely a word of the text. I have seen most of the layouts in something like their final form, but I have tried—much against my naturally interfering and not-all-that humble instincts—to refrain from influencing the choice of photos and the impression the layouts would convey. Naturally there were things here and there I was tempted to insist on altering, but my restraint at least allows me to disavow the editors' choices of any unflattering photos of friends, and to feel that the work is what I wanted it to be from the start: a critical and analytic—but not unfriendly—biography (and autobiography). In other words, this book is "authorized" in the sense that I approved wholeheartedly of its creators and delegated to them the right to make unfettered decisions on its content. But the only part for which I am directly responsible is the chronology of my life and career at the back of the book; if there are mistakes there, the blame is mine.

As the book took shape I began to see that it could well prove to have broader significance than I had first thought. Because of our tastes, temperaments, and circumstances, my father's life and my own have touched on and been touched by some of the most interesting people and events of this century. Aside from our own successes and failures, and the way events affected us, the now neatly ordered pictorial record tells a story that covers—however impressionistically—a lot of ground.

Whatever the book's origin, I am, I suppose, ultimately responsible for its existence, even if not for the form it takes. And it has taken on a more personal meaning for me than I had imagined it would. Over the year or more of its compilation I have become far more aware of being the last to bear the Fairbanks name. My father, and my mother as well, would, I think, have approved of my agreeing to the publication of this record of our overlapping histories. We chose different methods of dealing with the problems and pressures of public life, but my method was surely conditioned by my father's experience—and both, I daresay, have their interest for students of such matters.

My father and I became truly close and trusted friends only in the last eight or nine years of his life. However shy of each other we had been before, however disapproving he had been of me in my earlier years, he had never been consciously unkind to me. Or to anyone for that matter. Although more of an extrovert by nature than I, he was admittedly embarrassed by any outward demonstration of affection between us. Nevertheless, his basic "niceness" would often escape in the form of some sudden, circumspect gesture. As an example, the present from him I most treasure was one he gave me in my early twenties, at a time when he felt I had made it on my own. It is a very handsome cigarette case, but I treasure it for the inscription he wrote in it. In a facsimile of his own handwriting is a not-too-bad pun: "Just another case of father to son." That was all, but I recognized the sentiment behind it. He was a man who for years had, to my naturally prejudiced mind, set a splendid example—not just to me but to the world—to irresistible optimism and vitality, and a love of all life could offer. That was the heritage he was attempting to convey with his little gift. Following his death, my own life expanded in a number of ways that I think would have intrigued his vivid imagination and, I hope, pleased the author of that inscription. This photo-saga of our two lives is in many ways one continuous, continuing story—beginning with him. Hence, as the one who provided most of the material for it, I could, with respectful and grateful affection, paraphrase his own pun: "Just another record of son to father."

INTRODUCTION

IN THE SPRING OF 1975 I traveled down to Washington to visit Douglas Fairbanks, Jr. The reason for the journey was business having to do with this book, but that was only an excuse—we probably could have conducted it as well by phone or mail. What really impelled me was curiosity. Douglas was appearing at the Kennedy Center in a revival of Noel Coward's *Present Laughter* and I had never seen him act on stage and wanted very much to see if his modesty about the present state of his performing gift, which has always struck me as excessive to the point of falsity, was justified.

He makes it difficult for theatrically knowledgeable people to check up on him. They, of course, are located in places like New York and London, and he steadfastly refuses to appear before them, very simply because, as he once admitted to me, he is afraid to do so. Instead, he works the outlands, typically playing eight, ten, twelve weeks a year in vehicles that do not tax him very much and in which his charm, enhanced by our growing nostalgia about actors of his generation, can sweep away any reservations we might have about his skills.

This reticence I have always found curious, the more so since seeing him in *Present Laughter.* As anyone who remembers him in the light comedies he frequently made in Hollywood during the 1930s might imagine, he remains an able and charming presence in a drawing room, deft and graceful, with a good sense of comic timing and a way of imposing himself on his material and his audience without seeming to do so. He is careful and canny about not wearing out the warm welcome people are inclined to give him for old time's sake if for nothing else. Moreover, his remains a name to conjure with. Combined with Coward's—in whose work there is now a justifiably renewed interest—it was sufficient to draw full houses nearly every night of a run that was extended until if finally broke the Kennedy Center record. Olivier he isn't, but he never aspired to be, and within the limits that are imposed on a performer—partly by the nature of his talent, partly by the expectations an audience, conditioned by past experiences with him, brings to the theater—there is no rational reason why Douglas should not play Broadway or the West End anytime he feels like it. There are, however, other reasons, based on history and the way his personality has been shaped by it, responded to it, which account for his residence—now a couple of decades in length—on the fringes of show business rather than at its center. In a sense, that is what this book is about.

IT IS NOT STRICTLY TRUE that Douglas Elton Fairbanks, Jr. was born famous. When he came into the world on December 9, 1909, his father was, to be sure, locally well known as a reliable light leading man on Broadway, an actor with a following and a career still on the rise. It is true, however, that by the time his only child attained consciousness of himself and his place in the world, the father was well on his way to becoming a world figure of an unprecedented sort, what we have now taken to calling a superstar.

The instrument of his transformation was an infant industry called the movies. Prospering legit stars had eschewed films during the first decade of their existence, for to appear in these little ten-minute productions, silent and anonymous, was to publicly admit that your career was in such disarray that five or ten dollars—the going day rate for movie performers—was a significant sum to you. For a complex of reasons, however, that began to change around 1910. D. W. Griffith had, by that time, spent a couple of years as director at the Biograph studios, and his ambitions for himself—a lifelong failure as actor, playwright, poet—he had transferred to the new medium, devising a basic grammar for it which unlocked the power that had been implicit in films from the beginning. He also began adapting material from more respectable sources—the novel, the stage, even epic poetry—for the screen, giving it a new cachet. Equally significant, the public had begun singling out the anonymous players who appealed to it, trying to find out who they were, what they were really like, and a few industry leaders saw in this interest a way of building reliable markets for their products. It became clear to them that some mysteriously favored personalities were more important to audiences than the stories they appeared in, that if you advertised the presence of these individuals you could draw people to the theater no matter what the title or plot of the piece in which they were appearing. These stars, obviously, were worth almost any amount they cared to demand, so magical was their effect on a film's gross revenues. Finally, from 1912 (when the first European productions of something like modern feature length began appearing in the U.S.) to 1914 (when Griffith made his epochal *Birth of a Nation*) the trend toward longer pictures grew, and this meant a gain in respectability, too. Stories and characterizations could be developed in greater detail and, obviously, something that took an hour or even two to unfold on the screen could not be so easily dismissed as the cheap, short films had been by the nation's cultural arbiters.

All of this meant that stage performers started to change their minds about working in films, and by the spring of 1915, when Douglas Fairbanks, Sr. signed his first movie contract (for $2000 a week), Broadway stars were heading westward by the carload, like so many miners responding to tales of a new mother lode.

The majority of them did not succeed in the movies. The broad, pantomimic style of the stage at that time looked false to the intimately observing camera. It also revealed age in a way that was, compared to stage—where the actor was able to keep his distance from onlookers—cruel. Finally, since the movies were silent, actors were robbed of the instrument that had enabled many of them to override physical defects, compel the awed attention of an age that treasured the roundly spoken word, the voice. This new world belonged to the young, to those not locked by habit into the conventions of theatrical presentation of the self. It belonged, in short, to people rather like Douglas Fairbanks.

He had, God knows, his limits as an actor. In particular he seemed not to trust his face and tended to over-employ it, generally using more, and broader, expressions than he required to get his points across. On the other hand, he was such a wonderfully exuberant fellow that this unnatural vivacity seemed somehow natural to him. And anyway, it was not his face that people came to see, it was his body, his body in action, that charmed the public.

It had been his fortune since he was a boy in Denver. Even then, to borrow a thought from Alistair Cooke,* he had possessed, been possessed by, a spontaneous ability and desire to turn the world into a gymnasium. As a very young child, according to family legend, he had been a withdrawn and remarkably sober child. Once he discovered that he could attract attention by clambering dangerously up trees and porch lattices, by sailing heart-stoppingly off the garage roof, he was a changed boy, a show-off. And it was natural that his mother, deserted by his father, should try to channel his instinctive desire to be a show-off into the one outlet from which profit and at least a modicum of self-respect might be derived, namely the theater. Acting classes, a stint with a touring Shakespearean company, small parts on Broadway and on the road—this was his apprenticeship. And it never quite satisfied his athleticism. He was always proposing that he make an entrance walking on his hands or swinging down from a balcony. Despite his growing reputation in the theater, it was probably a good thing that the movies were invented in time for him to take advantage of them. Even the spectacle stage, to which he was not attracted, could not really have accommodated his energy, his obsession with stunting, with intricately choreographed movement.

With a little help from friends like directors Allan Dwan and John Emerson and writer Anita Loos (and the grudging acquiescence of Griffith, who couldn't figure out what to do with Doug, but was glad enough to have somebody else think of something to do with him), he concocted a wonderful screen character, a character who, in fact, endlessly found himself in a position to undergo the sort of transformation Douglas had himself enjoyed as a boy. He was usually introduced as a laughing-stock of some sort—the fatuous heir to a great fortune, perhaps, or alternatively, a dreamy youth trapped behind a clerkish counter and hoping against hope for the opportunity to escape. No matter, events were made to conspire in such a way that the inherent intelligence and courage of such a character was forced to emerge, permitting him to prove himself to those who had doubted him, sneered at him in the early reels.

*In his distinguished study, *Douglas Fairbanks: The Making of a Screen Character* (The Museum of Modern Art, 1940).

Sometimes explicitly, sometimes implicitly, these stories said something to audiences about the promise of American life. In a free and open society, they said, anybody could be anything he wanted if only he made a few breaks for himself—or even if he merely kept an eye open and took advantage of circumstances as they presented themselves. It was very comforting, a message the nation was ready for in the teens of this century, when the old world, a world of rigid caste and class, was committing slow suicide in the trenches of France. By the time America entered the war Douglas Fairbanks, with his comical, good-natured adventurousness, seemed to many people an archetypal representation of what was best in the American spirit. He was even writing books and magazine articles—or at least causing them to be written for his signature—setting forth his optimistic philosophy (*Laugh and Live* was his first title).

Laugh and Live

Laugh and Live

By
DOUGLAS FAIRBANKS

ILLUSTRATED

NEW YORK
BRITTON PUBLISHING COMPANY

And, indeed, his own life seemed to prove the truth of what he was saying on screen and off. In a matter of years and no more than a score of films, he had joined two early-comers, Charles Chaplin and Mary Pickford, at the pinnacle of his profession—stars that far outshone any others in the movie firmament. By 1918 he was his own producer and a force in the industry. The poor kid, with the psychologically messy childhood, had arrived not just at success, but at a fame and a fortune that was entirely unprecedented in the long history of theatrical performance. For the movies were, truly, the first mass medium. In the past it had taken an actor years to establish himself, to tour long enough in some identity-establishing role to become well known to an audience large enough to be defined as a mass. A movie actor could do so in a matter of weeks as hundreds of prints were distributed simultaneously to exchanges and theaters throughout the world. It was now possible to be "discovered" in a moment by millions of people, to become, almost literally overnight, the focus of everyone's attention. They talked—and they listened to themselves talk—and quite unconsciously this growing buzz magnified interest in, the importance of, the players they talked about.

Moreover, these players appeared not as tiny, distant figures on a stage. They appeared magnified many times life size on the screen, and one felt that one knew them in a new, intimate way, that in fancy they were our friends, people we could address on a first-name basis. The press, of course, catered to the insatiable desire for information about their private lives, the kind of stuff one does, indeed, know about one's good friends. A whole new branch of journalism, the fan publications, was created to cater to this need. What we had here, as I have argued elsewhere in more detail,* was the birth of the modern celebrity system, the beginnings of a new definition of what it meant to be famous.

*In *His Picture in the Papers* (New York: Charterhouse, 1974), a longer biographical essay about the elder Fairbanks.

A *system?* Yes, I think so. It was not in the beginning, and it is not now, a well-articulated or entirely reasonable system. In some ways it defies analysis. Yet certain generalizations can be made about it. The first of these is that its chief beneficiary-victims can—indeed, must—nominate themselves for central status in the system by their choice of profession (actors, athletes, politicians, occasional artists and intellectuals willing to play the fame game as, for instance, Norman Mailer has) and can campaign for public favor in a hundred ways. But the very top—the place where legends live and never die—is achieved by accident, because the person achieving it first of all matches, perhaps slightly exaggerates, current standards of physical attractiveness, seems to project certain traits of personality deemed, at the moment of his or her arrival in mass awareness, desirable, not to say enviable. The movies, and then the other media as they came into being or adapted (as the press did) over the years, acted as a sort of bullhorn *cum* telephoto lens, magnifying and multiplying the images of these chosen few, not merely in the medium where they found their basic employment, but *everywhere,* so that they became inescapable symbols of the spirit of their time. Eventually, of course, their famousness detached itself from whatever achievements had brought them to attention in the first place, became a thing quite unto itself.

At that point they perforce underwent—and this usually came quite by surprise to the individual, no matter how many others it had happened to before—a radical change in their way of life. They discovered they could not move freely through the world, that they required protection from the multitudes whose passionate interest in them could sometimes prove dangerous to them physically, was always an annoying intrusion. They required entourages to protect them, to run the errands they could no longer casually undertake. They also required resorts, restaurants, transportation where their privacy could be assured and where, needless to say, they were likely to encounter only their peers on the celebrity status ladder. All of this, naturally, served to further titillate public interest in their comings and goings (and to add a note of envy to the brew). It also served to cut them off from their roots, from their instinctive sense of the attitudes and preoccupations of their audience, on whose favor, of course, they still depended, not perhaps for their livelihoods—since stars in show biz tend to get rich very quickly and, if they are the least bit intelligent, tend to stay that way, contrary to popular fantasies—but for emotional sustenance.

All of this is fairly easy to see now, to make easy generalizations about. But Fairbanks, along with his best friend, Chaplin, and his second wife, Pickford, were the first to learn about it, were forced, under the impress of fast-moving events, to improvise their answers (the pictures of Doug and Mary being mobbed in Europe on their wedding trip are proof, if any is needed, that no one was prepared for the kind of mass curiosity, mass adulation, that greeted them everywhere). The simple need for police protection when a celebrity comes down from the screen to pass among the people was not understood in those early days. And if the need for so primitive a precaution was not understood, how much else was not understood by the principals in this business and their advisors?

Henry Ford looks somber, but he accepted Doug's challenge to climb to the roof of his house. Edsel Ford is at right.

Conferring with Eddie Rickenbacker. Fairbanks put on a Wild West show for the returning Ace.

The answer is, obviously, a great deal. Pickford, for example, tended as the years went on to withdraw more and more to the house at the top of the best hill in Beverly Hills, the house dubbed "Pickfair" by the press. Chaplin, for his part, more and more cast himself off-screen as a traditionally defined artist (and artist of genius, at that)—inscrutable, unpredictable, often outrageous, more often pretentious, very much a loner, the author of everything about his films, including the music. Of the three, it was Fairbanks who truly enjoyed celebrity, who restlessly traveled the globe, his name and fame an entree to social, intellectual, artistic circles of every sort, a man who, at the height of his powers, manifestly enjoyed being recognized, enjoyed his wealth and every facet of the business that produced that wealth. I am convinced that though he did not consciously recognize the fact that his was a new occupation ("celebrity," not "actor" or even "star"), he was unconsciously aware of it, and dealing with it, in every aspect of his life—at least when he was on the rise. He was to become a hurt, puzzled, depressed human being when, sound and middle age arriving simultaneously in his life, he found himself slipping and unable to imagine what he should do about it.

THE QUESTION IS, "WHY HIM?" That is to say, why of all the new stars of the new medium was it Fairbanks who seemed most aware of what was happening to him, best able to master the new forces playing on, playing with, his life and thus derive from them the pleasure that seems to glow from his face in nearly every picture in the early sections of this book?

The simple answer to those questions is that Douglas Fairbanks, Sr. had always been ambitious for something other than mere fame and money, that he had been, from the start, to put it bluntly, a climber. Even as a young Broadway actor he had hung out with socialites and his first marriage, to Beth Sully, the mother of his only child, had been a "good" marriage—into a family of wealth and a certain amount of social prestige. Her father, Daniel (known to the press as "the Cotton King"), was of that class of entrepreneurs and manipulators who acceded to power in the great age of industrial expansion following the Civil War and whose new money, freely spent, gilded the age or turned it mauve, depending on your choice of social commentators. By the time Fairbanks—the classic provincial making good in the capital—took Beth's hand, a certain patina of age had surrounded the Sully money and the family moved in excellent circles. It was scarcely Fairbanks' fault that the old boy lost it all—or most of it—and that he had to help support the Sullys, as his son would a little later.

This is not to imply that he did not love Beth Sully; it was merely convenient that besides being attractive she offered him excellent connections in social realms actors are sometimes invited to visit, but rarely to enter fully. Nor does one wish to imply that he did not love Mary Pickford when he began so passionately to pursue her, when he abandoned Beth to marry her. It was, however, a convenient coincidence—and a career coup—that the leading male star of the moment could join forces with the leading female star of the day, creating a nexus of power that caused the formation of one major corporation (United Artists) and a social force of unparalleled potency. Some doors might have remained closed to him alone; none could resist their combined force. Royalty, nobility, the great artists, athletes, political figures, all rub shoulders in these pages as they did in the life of the first of our two protagonists. And having spent many weeks poring through tens of thousands of pictures to make the selection we here present, I must say that I find the life of Pickfair, the Fairbanks studio, the Fairbankses on tour, utterly enviable. Why deny it? The elder Fairbanks knew everyone who was anyone and was able to be easy with them all—Jack Dempsey and the Prince of Wales, Somerset Maugham and a young politician whom he thought had the stuff for a career in the producing end of show business, Franklin D. Roosevelt. Terrific! Why deny it? A good time was being had here and I see no reason to be dour or moralistic about it. One can try to understand it without disapproving it. Which of us, thrust into Fairbanks' position, would have done otherwise (assuming we had his gift for turning on the charm)? Can we really say that Chaplin, doubtless the superior artist, had in the last analysis, a better life, a life we would wish to emulate?

HAVING SAID ALL THAT, however, one must note the human costs of Fairbanks' endeavor, and here we begin to circle back to his son. He was but nine years old when his parents separated, not an easy business, as everyone knows, for a child to deal with. In his case, however, his father, with so much of his career, and more than that, his very essence, staked on perpetual youthfulness, made it quite clear that he wished his son had never been born. Especially, one imagines, he wished he had not indulged his vanity by naming the boy after himself, for if his namesake started turning up in the papers, everyone would be reminded immediately of the more famous bearer of the name, start speculating on how old he must be if his son were approaching manhood. And, as it turned out, Junior was going to approach manhood not in some out-of-the-way prep school, some quiet college, but in his father's very own playground, the movies.

What happened was that Beth Sully, having made an unhappy rebound marriage that broke up rather quickly, attempted to run her lump sum divorce settlement into a larger amount in the stock market and instead saw it dwindle alarmingly. She and her son retreated to Europe, hoping—just like the expatriate artists of the twenties—to stretch their resources because of the favorable rate of exchange American currency enjoyed there. It was not long before Beth was, as her son likes to put it, "popping a jewel every now and then" in order to make ends meet. Thus when Jesse Lasky—an old rival of his father's—stepped forward to offer the boy a movie contract, mother and son had to be interested. They knew that though Douglas had shed the puppy fat that had so offended his father and was a handsome youth, Lasky was not buying looks, he was buying a name, a name that was bound to evoke curiosity among the public, therefore money at the box office. That he could also tweak the lion of his industry's tail while taking this very reasonable gamble only pleased Lasky the more, wicked fellow.

Fairbanks, Jr. still paints and sculpts skillfully, and daughter Victoria shows the family talent.

The senior Fairbanks raged and sulked and put pressure on friends not to aid and abet his son's acting career—we know that. But what about the young man himself? What an awkward position he was in! Like most kids the idea of being a "movie star" appealed to him and, of course, the thought that he could ease the financial plight of his mother and her family had its appeal, too. The fantasy of being the man of the family, the provider, at a precocious age, often occurs to boys of every station.

On the other hand, Douglas, Jr. had manifested no particular interest in following in his father's footsteps. If he had a youthful gift, it was for painting and drawing, in which he received lessons and showed some talent. Moreover, in normal circumstances he would have had years to make a final choice of career, and if we can extrapolate backward from his later activities, might well have chosen business or diplomacy or even the military and thus escaped what is surely the curse of his life (though he has never said as much to me)—the endless comparisons and contrasts with his father. However, the circumstances were not normal,* and Douglas Fairbanks, Jr. became an actor. His first picture, *Stephen Steps Out,* was not a conspicuous success, and soon enough he was reduced by the studio to playing small parts in minor films, usually getting his best roles when he was loaned out to other producers. Worse, he was expected to do just about anything the studio required of him—write titles, serve as a camera assistant, undertake all sorts of menial, if not downright demeaning, activities. The contrast between his toilings and his father's grandiose activities—he now made just one film a year, an expensive romantic action spectacular, in which he indulged his lavish tastes in décor and costume—could not have been more stark. And though Mary Pickford did her best to soften Senior's attitude toward his son, and though he was erratically generous with the boy, these cannot have been happy years for Douglas, Jr. It has always seemed to me that his ambivalence toward acting must have its roots in this time, when its pleasures were few, its rewards modest, and the general, uninformed belief that he was trying to cash in on his father's reputation.

If he had had a divine passion for his art, things might have been different for him, this period of apprenticeship a time to be recalled with humorous fondness. But that is a note he rarely strikes. It was a job, and since he was intelligent he learned to do it well, with a certain developing flair. But it was impossible for him to see acting as a great calling, something to devote oneself to with the religious fervor young people, more innocent than he was about the ways of show biz, often do.

Certainly his father's example was less than inspiring to him. He knew, firsthand, the dark side of Senior's character: the brooding depressions that could last for days, the restless need for escape which lay beneath his endless travels, an unstable driving force beneath these seemingly glamorous peregrinations. As a reasonable young man, and a frequent victim of his father's erratic moods, he had no reason to suppose that even great success in the profession that had been chosen for him would bring a great deal of happiness or fulfillment.

Moreover, as the twenties turned into the thirties and his own career began to prosper—his voice, so much better suited to sound films than his father's was, gave him an opportunity to establish his own identity more firmly—he had reason to see how transitory even unprecedented success could be. For his father was now floundering desperately, unable to make either the charming comedies of his early phases or to sustain the kind of expensive historical spectacles, mythic and magical in overtone, which had distinguished his career, given it uniqueness, in the early and middle twenties. His youth gone, the youth that he had dared not think would ever end, the elder Fairbanks became, increasingly, a rather pathetic figure. He allowed his production standards to slip and he offered careless, slapdash films, entirely out of touch both with new times

*It seems odd that Douglas, Sr. did not simply make a cash offer to his former wife, since he had plenty of it, to ease her difficulties and keep his son off the screen; perhaps, with his rather Victorian sense of honor, this smacked of blackmail to him.

and his own talents. If anything, the pace of his travels increased as he searched frantically for something, anything, to arrest his attention, occupy his mind. He continued to be seen at all the best places, with all the best people, to announce great plans to become a full-time producer, but mostly it would seem, he played golf and pursued women who offered temporary reassurance that his manhood, threatened by the failure of his career, was still intact. As he neared 50 he told his son that he could discover no reason to get up in the morning. "I've done everything," he said—"twice." He wanted, he said, to die quickly.

Was this, then, what the star's life offered, the young man must surely have asked himself. A brief moment—only about a dozen years in his father's case—of fun and prosperity, to be followed by decades of regretful anticlimax. If so, shouldn't one withhold some part of oneself from total emotional commitment to this art? Shouldn't one, perhaps, prepare fall-back positions so as not to be caught out as his father now was, so that one could retire gracefully from the center of the stage, thus avoiding the pain of being seen a fool? One senses in Douglas Fairbanks, Jr., both on stage and in private, something held back, some caution in his behavior. His wife, Mary Lee, once told a biographer that he acts like a guest at his own parties, and that is the way he seems to me to move through most of life—tentative, fussy, vague, careful not to impose or to be imposed upon—careful, in short, not to be like his father. It is why, I think, he has chosen to be, in the last couple of decades, what might be called "a gentleman actor." He prefers his friends to believe, prefers himself to believe, that his occasional stage and television appearances are a sort of harmless hobby or even foible, nothing to be taken seriously, nothing that he himself takes seriously, though—as his Washington appearance proved—his actual work is carefully prepared, crisply delivered, totally professional.

At the beginning of a close friendship.

Here, ambiguity must enter our consideration of Fairbanks' life and work as a performer. As his career began to prosper in the early thirties, as the influence of his ambitious first wife, Joan Crawford, began to exert itself, as he grew—finally—closer to his father, who required the emotional stability of his trustworthy, objective-minded son, he began himself to enjoy some of the pleasures of being well known, of being, if never the superstar his father had been, then certainly a solidly established name above the title. There had always been something romantic in his nature and he enjoyed the dash and romance of the roles he played, enjoyed, as he admits, the boyish pleasures of dressing up in splendid finery—a taste which continues to this day, any occasion requiring him to wear a uniform (he is a retired Captain in the Naval Reserve) or his decorations pleasing him. More important, he learned to relish the small attentions, the pleasant perks that go along with being well known. And spending a great deal of time in England during the early and middle years of the thirties, he found the entree his name provided into Mayfair society extremely gratifying. Unwillingly, unwittingly perhaps, he found himself, despite what seems to me a genuine shyness, hooked on the ego-stroking rewards of celebrity. The experience was not as overpowering for him as it had been for his father—he was not a star of the same magnitude and, besides, close observation of his father's life had armored him against the dangers to which the older man had succumbed. At some point in this period Douglas, Jr. surely resolved not to stumble blindly and miserably from the stage as his father was doing, resolved not to self-destruct.

Prematurely, perhaps, he decided he must be his own producer, his experiences as a contract player in Hollywood having ended rather disappointingly and having a strong, very American desire to be something more than a mere actor, an occupation which is often regarded as not entirely manly in this country—compared with meeting a payroll, anyway. That is why so many of our movie stars have insisted on forming their own companies, running their own careers. It did not work out awfully well for Douglas, Jr. The pictures he made in England in 1935 and '36 were not, as a group, profitable, and it was working for others, notably in *The Prisoner of Zenda* and *Gunga Din,* back home, that he established himself anew as a solid box-office figure.

IRONICALLY, IT WAS THE WAR that allowed the younger Fairbanks to finally establish himself, in his own eyes, as his own man, in no way beholden to his father and, after his father's death in 1939, with no need, either, to revolt against him. The ties he had forged in England in the 1930s made him extraordinarily sympathetic to that nation's plight when, with France, it stood naked and seemingly defenseless against Hitler. He was appalled by isolationist sentiment in the U.S., determined to use his influence, his star's presence, to enlist support for a nation he believed to be our natural ally and one which, sooner or later, we would have to join in stopping Germany. The issues of that moment—lifting the embargo on arms shipments to friendly nations, lending destroyers to Britain to replace ships lost to U-boats, establishing Lend-Lease, now seem remote, but the passion of the debate between internationalists and isolationists was not. It required enormous moral courage for an actor, a man dependent for his livelihood on—at the very least—being inoffensive to the largest possible number of people, to take sides in it publicly. Here was a way to utilize the connections of two lifetimes in order to make his concern manifest.

Connectedness is, indeed, one of the sub-texts of this volume, these lives. One notes, for example, that in 1920, when the S.S. *Olympic* sailed from London on one of its July crossings it carried not only Doug and Mary returning from their first European tour, but a young vaudeville trouper named Archie Leach, who, as Cary Grant, was to become the friend and co-star of

Douglas, Jr.* More to the present point, on visiting the White House as a representative of (among other activities) the interventionist Committee to Aid the Allies, at whose rallies he was often the principal speaker and drawing card, young Fairbanks would find his father's old friend and scenarist, Robert Sherwood, now serving as a writer for Franklin Roosevelt. Roosevelt, of course, had been an acquaintance since the elder Fairbanks had been a devoted salesman of Liberty Bonds during World War I. Across the water, once he became a naval officer, Fairbanks would serve under Louis ("Dickie") Mountbatten, chief of combined operations and a friend since he passed part of his honeymoon at Pickfair when Fairbanks, Jr. was in his teens.

And so on. These men introduced the younger Fairbanks to the corridors of political power, where he had to fight against figurehead assignments, where he was challenged to prove himself as a man to be taken seriously. Here, at last, was man's work—and work entirely different from any his father had undertaken. It is no wonder that he neglected his film career for this heady, novel atmosphere.

And yet, of course, he would not prove himself until he could lay to rest the isolationist jibes that he did not understand the difference between real war and back-lot representations of it. So he joined the Naval Reserve and went on active duty in the fall prior to Pearl Harbor. And he had, as they say, a good war. He served on the *Wasp,* delivering Spitfires to beleaguered Malta, made the Murmansk run, commanded small boat actions off Italy, Yugoslavia, the South of France, proving himself a resourceful tactician and, most important, a genuinely brave man.

It was the experience of his life. It changed him in some profound way. He could never again be merely an actor, especially an actor on hire. He must keep up his connections with the world of affairs. So he retained his commission, eventually rising to a captaincy in the Reserve, made himself ever available for official and unofficial diplomatic roles, and, of course, insisted on being a businessman, too. He was his own producer once again on a series of post-war films and of the early, long-running anthology series he made for TV. In addition, he worked on enterprises that had nothing to do with the theatrical professions. And, his resources having been drained by his long wartime service, he re-established himself in comfortable economic circumstances.

Yet he became rather an enigmatic figure. One wonders where he belongs, where he thinks he belongs. He is visible enough as a performer to maintain that identity with the general public, relentlessly active in his other capacities, so that his contact in the other worlds he touches are always in good order. He himself says that all this action is the result of "the almost subconscious determination to 'prove' myself, to give the lie to all those who plagued my childhood and youth with, 'you never will . . . you never can . . . you wouldn't dare.'" He seems quite content—and determinedly busy.

*Grant's recollections of that passage have recently been unearthed by Pauline Kael: "Once even I found myself being photographed with Mr. Fairbanks during a game of shuffleboard. As I stood beside him, I tried with shy, inadequate words to tell him of my adulation. He was a splendidly trained athlete and acrobat [as was Leach], affable and warmed by success and well-being. A gentleman in the true sense of the word. . . . It suddenly dawns on me as this is being written that I've doggedly striven to keep tanned ever since, only because of a desire to emulate his healthful appearance."

Yet there remains something elusive about him. I find, despite a genuine fondness that has developed in me since he responded, unbidden, with great generosity, to an article, then a book, I wrote about his father, it is impossible to find the true center of the man. Unfailing courtesy, a rich fund of (and gift for telling) anecdotes—these are omnipresent. But he hates to openly admit to his needs and desires. He likes to "cause" things to happen without seeming to, and becomes quite hurt when his guarded hints about the way he'd like things to go are not picked up, though he would rather die than openly suggest, let alone order, action. (This aspect of his character is very clearly visible when he takes a solo curtain call which, given his status, is his by right and custom. Yet when the moment comes, at the end of a performance, things are so arranged that a suddenly rising curtain seems to catch him unawares, making his way to the wings. Whereupon, registering modestly delighted surprise, he turns to face the audience and accept their tribute.)

Present Laughter: with Jane Alexander and old friend Ilka Chase, who appeared on screen with Fairbanks in *The Careless Age,* 1929.

Hard to figure all this. The son and heir to show business royalty, is his manner that of the sons and heirs of British society, with whom he has been friends for so long? Or is he still the shy little boy his father tried to hide in the closet and who must once have been hungry for approval yet afraid to ask openly for it, fearing rebuff? One must wonder, too, if finally his fragmented career—a little of this, a little of that, but fundamentally lacking in a full-scale commitment to anything, including himself—has not added to this insecurity, making him genuinely dubious about whether he is entitled, truly entitled, to any of the rewards he has received—including the small transitory one of our applause at the end of a show.

YET SOMEHOW ONE DOES NOT WANT to end this essay on that note. In gathering the material for this book from his and other archives one has been struck by his cool objectivity about what he has permitted one to select from, his refusal, upon looking over the layouts, to insist on the inclusion or the exclusion of anything. He has a curious ability to look on his own life objectively. Only two things is he insistently proud of. The first is that, as economic man, he has made his own way—accepting no help from his father or his father's friends, accepting, on several occasions (when he was starting out, when he fought with studios that had him under contract, when his first production ventures didn't work out, when his war services wiped out his resources), that he was broke and had only his own talent and wit to achieve, or re-achieve, security. The other is that his career has been validated objectively by the honors and awards he has received. He takes an almost boyish pleasure in his decorations, and he values the fact that people of world stature in realms of serious endeavor have sought out and value his friendship.

It was, I think, important to see him in Washington starring in his old friend Noel Coward's play. He treasured Coward's friendship greatly, and admired his well-concealed industriousness, his good counsel and, above all, his courage. "When fate was unusually rough with him (as it so often was) or when he suffered severe setbacks to his normally good health, one never, *never* heard a word of complaint. He was encouraging to rivals, contemporaries, or beginners, and one of the most loyal people, in or out of the theater, I've known." Now here was Fairbanks, having a gratifying success playing a part Coward had written autobiographically—and quite unsparingly—in Washington, which is full of old friends from Navy days and before. There were parties, it seemed, almost every night—at the White House, at various embassies. One weekend he was invited out to Chadd's Ford to visit Andrew Wyeth. The painter's father, the famous illustrator N. C. Wyeth, had been an admirer of, and an influence on, Fairbanks' father, who had returned the favor. The sons had corresponded but never met, and their meeting quite obviously warmed Douglas. The whole experience, indeed, seemed to represent a kind of culmination for him. For once, all the elements that have made up his life until now coalesced in a confirmatory way. Like Coward, he has never been a man to complain about anything, but this time he seemed to me particularly easy with himself, particularly open and content. Everything seemed to make sense for him—and for me, watching and listening.

Andrew Wyeth shows off newly acquired skills to a pro.

The form this book has taken is an attempt to catch and hold that mood, to permit people to see in the visible record of these two linked lives, unique in the fact that they span the entire modern history of celebrity, what it was like not just to be Fairbankses (interesting enough), but what it has been like to be famous in our age. There is much pleasure and some pain in the pictures that follow—and nearly all of them are pictures whose composition was conditioned by the avidity with which we followed these lives, attempted, in fact, to live vicariously through them. We are the photographers as well as the viewers of these pictures, and we, it seems to me, bear a share of responsibility for the life-styles recorded in them.

A Star Is Born

Progenitors: H. (for Hezekiah) Charles Ulman was the scion of a wealthy Pennsylvania family, a prominent New York lawyer, a founder of the nation's first bar association, a Union officer during the Civil War. He met the former Ella Adelaide Marsh, of New Orleans, when he helped settle her affairs after the sudden death of her first husband, John Fairbanks, and obtained her divorce after a disastrous second marriage—in the process winning her affections. They settled in Denver, where an increasingly restless Ulman pursued both a legal career and a gold strike—unsuccessfully. Their children, Robert and Douglas (opposite), arrived in 1882 and '83. Five years later H. Charles decamped to become a paid speaker for Benjamin Harrison's presidential campaign. He never returned—except to cadge drinking money from Douglas after he became a stage star.

Clements
1617 Champa St.
Denver, Colo.

Charles Ulman's middle-aged restlessness—and moodiness—would, in time, settle on his second son. Despite the sobriety exhibited in the formal portrait opposite, the lad's first inheritance was Ulman's theatricality of temperament. The old man was proud of his friendship with—and physical resemblance to—Edwin Booth. The boy had a natural gift for mimicry and a delight in showing off, usually with physically daring pranks. Below, the program of his first public appearance, at a demonstration by Margaret Fealy's acting classes. It was his mother, incidentally, who insisted on changing the family name back to that of her first husband—a measure of her bitterness over the failure of her later marriages.

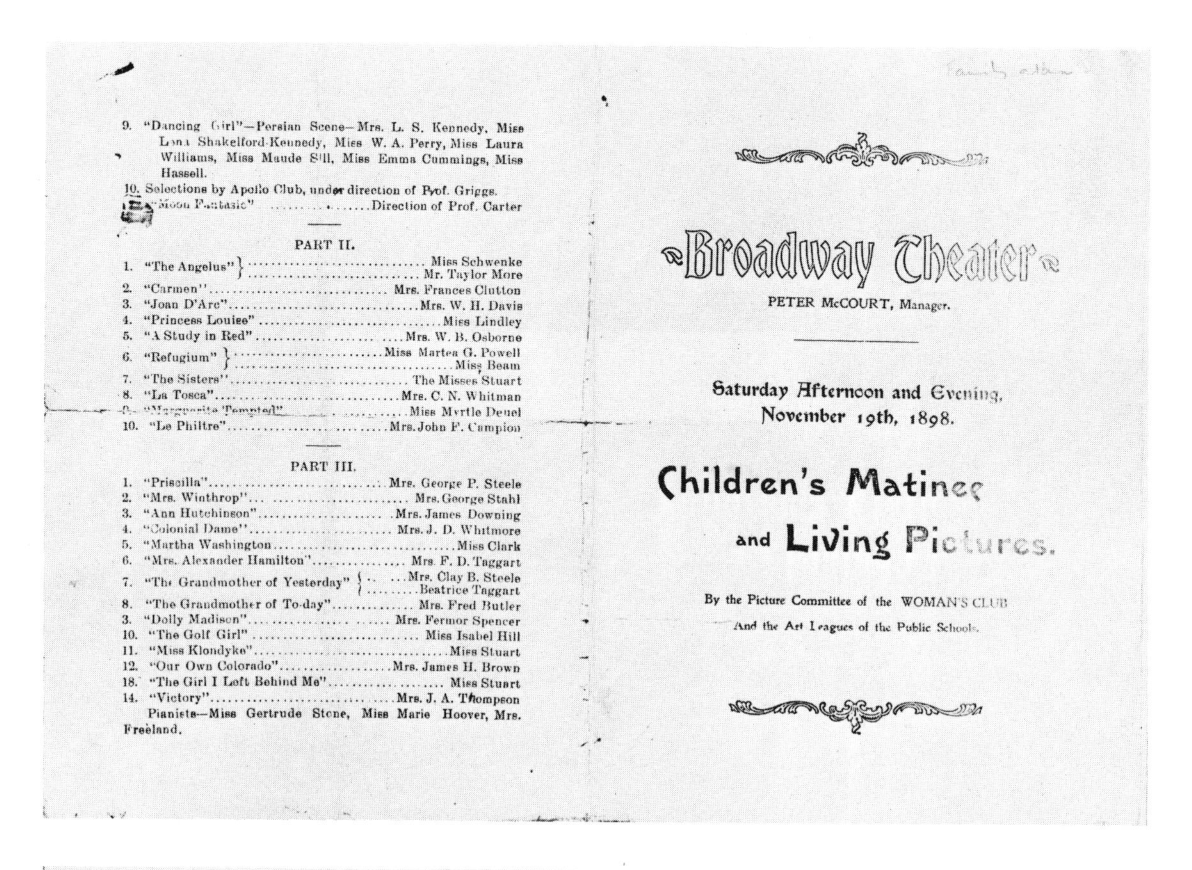

9. "Dancing Girl"—Persian Scene—Mrs. L. S. Kennedy, Miss Lena Shakelford-Kennedy, Miss W. A. Perry, Miss Laura Williams, Miss Maude Sill, Miss Emma Cummings, Miss Hassell.

10. Selections by Apollo Club, under direction of Prof. Griggs.

"Moon Fantastic" ....Direction of Prof. Carter

PART II.

1. "The Angelus" .... Miss Schwenke / Mr. Taylor More
2. "Carmen" .... Mrs. Frances Clutton
3. "Joan D'Arc" .... Mrs. W. H. Davis
4. "Princess Louise" .... Miss Lindley
5. "A Study in Red" .... Mrs. W. B. Osborne
6. "Refugium" .... Miss Martea G. Powell / Miss Beam
7. "The Sisters" .... The Misses Stuart
8. "La Tosca" .... Mrs. C. N. Whitman
9. "Marguerite Tempted" .... Miss Myrtle Deuel
10. "Le Philtre" .... Mrs. John F. Campion

PART III.

1. "Priscilla" .... Mrs. George P. Steele
2. "Mrs. Winthrop" .... Mrs. George Stahl
3. "Ann Hutchinson" .... Mrs. James Downing
4. "Colonial Dame" .... Mrs. J. D. Whitmore
5. "Martha Washington .... Miss Clark
6. "Mrs. Alexander Hamilton" .... Mrs. F. D. Taggart
7. "The Grandmother of Yesterday" .... Mrs. Clay B. Steele / Beatrice Taggart
8. "The Grandmother of To-day" .... Mrs. Fred Butler
9. "Dolly Madison" .... Mrs. Fermor Spencer
10. "The Golf Girl" .... Miss Isabel Hill
11. "Miss Klondyke" .... Miss Stuart
12. "Our Own Colorado" .... Mrs. James H. Brown
13. "The Girl I Left Behind Me" .... Miss Stuart
14. "Victory" .... Mrs. J. A. Thompson

Pianists—Miss Gertrude Stone, Miss Marie Hoover, Mrs. Freeland.

Broadway Theater

PETER McCOURT, Manager.

Saturday Afternoon and Evening, November 19th, 1898.

Children's Matinee and Living Pictures.

By the Picture Committee of the WOMAN'S CLUB And the Art Leagues of the Public Schools.

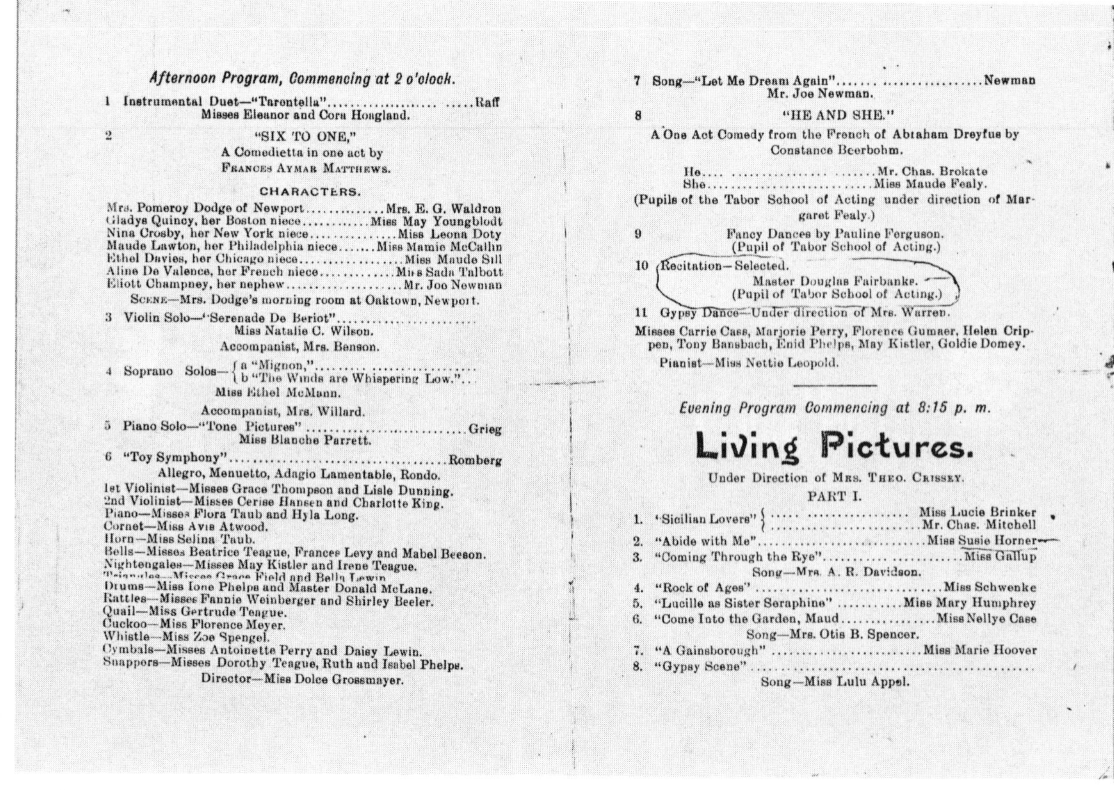

Afternoon Program, Commencing at 2 o'clock.

1 Instrumental Duet—"Tarentella" .... Raff
Misses Eleanor and Cora Hoagland.

2 "SIX TO ONE,"
A Comedietta in one act by
Frances Aymar Matthews.

CHARACTERS.

Mrs. Pomeroy Dodge of Newport .... Mrs. E. G. Waldron
Gladys Quincy, her Boston niece .... Miss May Youngbludt
Nina Crosby, her New York niece .... Miss Leona Doty
Maude Lawton, her Philadelphia niece .... Miss Mamie McCallin
Ethel Davies, her Chicago niece .... Miss Maude Sill
Aline De Valence, her French niece .... Miss Sadu Talbott
Eliott Champney, her nephew .... Mr. Joe Newman

Scene—Mrs. Dodge's morning room at Oaktown, Newport.

3 Violin Solo—"Serenade De Beriot" ....
Miss Natalie C. Wilson.
Accompanist, Mrs. Benson.

4 Soprano Solos—a "Mignon," .... b "The Winds are Whispering Low." ...
Miss Ethel McMann.
Accompanist, Mrs. Willard.

5 Piano Solo—"Tone Pictures" .... Grieg
Miss Blanche Parrett.

6 "Toy Symphony" .... Romberg
Allegro, Menuetto, Adagio Lamentable, Rondo.

1st Violinist—Misses Grace Thompson and Lisle Dunning.
2nd Violinist—Misses Cerise Hansen and Charlotte King.
Piano—Misses Flora Taub and Hyla Long.
Cornet—Miss Avis Atwood.
Horn—Miss Selina Taub.
Bells—Misses Beatrice Teague, Frances Levy and Mabel Beeson.
Nightengales—Misses May Kistler and Irene Teague.
Triangles—Misses Grace Field and Bella Lewin.
Drums—Miss Ione Phelps and Master Donald McLane.
Rattles—Misses Fannie Weinberger and Shirley Beeler.
Quail—Miss Gertrude Teague.
Cuckoo—Miss Florence Meyer.
Whistle—Miss Zoe Spengel.
Cymbals—Misses Antoinette Perry and Daisy Lewin.
Snappers—Misses Dorothy Teague, Ruth and Isabel Phelps.
Director—Miss Dolce Grossmayer.

7 Song—"Let Me Dream Again" .... Newman
Mr. Joe Newman.

8 "HE AND SHE."
A One Act Comedy from the French of Abraham Dreyfus by Constance Beerbohm.

He .... Mr. Chas. Brokate
She .... Miss Maude Fealy.

(Pupils of the Tabor School of Acting under direction of Margaret Fealy.)

9 Fancy Dances by Pauline Ferguson.
(Pupil of Tabor School of Acting.)

10 Recitation—Selected.
Master Douglas Fairbanks.
(Pupil of Tabor School of Acting.)

11 Gypsy Dance—Under direction of Mrs. Warren.

Misses Carrie Cass, Marjorie Perry, Florence Gumaer, Helen Crippen, Tony Bansbach, Enid Phelps, May Kistler, Goldie Domey.

Pianist—Miss Nettie Leopold.

Evening Program Commencing at 8:15 p. m.

Living Pictures.

Under Direction of Mrs. Theo. Crissey.

PART I.

1. "Sicilian Lovers" .... Miss Lucie Brinker / Mr. Chas. Mitchell
2. "Abide with Me" .... Miss Susie Horner
3. "Coming Through the Rye" .... Miss Gallup
Song—Mrs. A. R. Davidson.
4. "Rock of Ages" .... Miss Schwenke
5. "Lucille as Sister Seraphine" .... Miss Mary Humphrey
6. "Come Into the Garden, Maud .... Miss Nellye Case
Song—Mrs. Otis B. Spencer.
7. "A Gainsborough" .... Miss Marie Hoover
8. "Gypsy Scene" ....
Song—Miss Lulu Appel.

Fairbanks, so the story goes, deliberately got himself kicked out of school in order to go on the stage—joining touring star Frederic Warde's Shakespearean company in 1899. A year later he was on Broadway, but he vacillated between the stage and other activities for some years before Grace George, the actress who was married to producer William Brady, detected in him a star quality that led Brady to sign him to the long-term contract that gave his career drive and coherence. On this page at right, some of the many hats Fairbanks wore (or carried) during the 14 years when he was establishing himself as one of the theater's best light leading men: top, an early role in *The Reporter;* middle, as a bellboy, but his first lead, in 1905's *A Case of Frenzied Finance*—the beginning of the Brady build-up; bottom, the show that made him a star, *The Man of the Hour* (1906). Below left, with star-manager-writer Thomas Wise in *A Gentleman from Mississippi,* which preoccupied them in New York and on tour from 1909 to 1911. Opposite, an odd locale for a courtship with Millicent Evans in *The Cub* in 1912.

MR. DOUGLAS FAIRBANKS

DOUGLAS FAIRBANKS is generally regarded as the leading exponent of light comedy boys and young men of to-day. He has an ingratiating personality charged with health, directness, breeziness, and a certain patrician quality which contributes an attraction to any part he plays. He has been on the stage only nine years, yet in that time he has created a new rôle in New York on an average of at least once a year.

Mr. Fairbanks was born in Colorado and went on the stage in 1899, in support of Frederick Warde, playing small parts in that actor's Shakespearian repertoire. He soon doffed the romantic costume, however, and has since been seen only in modern dress. He made his début at the Manhattan Theatre in 1900, in support of Herbert Kelcey and Effie Shannon as the young lover, Lord Canning, in Martha Morton's "Her Lord and Master." The play passed and Fairbanks remained. The next season he acted small parts in "The Rose of Plymouth Town" and "Mrs. Jack."

Landry Court was the first character in which he had a real chance to score and he attained a fixed position by his performance of it. This was in Channing Pollock's dramatization of Frank Norris's "The Pit," in Wilton Lackaye's company in the spring of 1904. He played in "Two Little Sailor Boys," and when "Fantana" ran at the Lyric, he took his first and last dip into musical comedy.

The next time he appeared he was "featured" in "A Case of Frenzied Finance." It was not for long. A part in "As Ye Sow" reacquainted him with touring in 1905. During the summer of 1906 he acted a round of juvenile parts in one of the summer stock companies for which Denver has for many years been famous, and when he returned to New York in the fall he created Thomas Smith, Jr., with Grace George in "Clothes." Two of his most conspicuous hits sandwiched a failure in his successive appearances as Perry Carter Wainwright in "The Man of the Hour," as a star in "All for a Girl" and playing the secretary as a co-star with Thomas A. Wise in "A Gentleman From Mississippi."

IN "THE MAN OF THE HOUR"

IN "ALL FOR A GIRL"

IN "A GENTLEMAN FROM MISSISSIPPI"

IN "A CASE OF FRENZIED FINANCE"

A 1912 clipping from a theatrical journal attests to Fairbanks' eminence in his art—though no stage could really contain his boundless energy. He truly required the scope of the screen to employ his gifts fully. At right, the stage-struck heiress Beth Sully, who met him during the run of *The Man of the Hour.* They married July 11, 1907. Perhaps because of her family's prodding, perhaps because there were no worthwhile parts, he stayed away from the theater for almost a year, working for a soap company her father controlled.

Kenneth Ridge, at Watch Hill, Rhode Island, was the summer seat of Daniel Sully and site of the Fairbanks-Sully nuptials. Its master, Daniel Sully, was known variously as "the Cotton King" (having once cornered the market in that commodity) and as the "Savior of the South"—for driving the price of cotton up. In 1904 he declared himself bankrupt by around three million dollars and his legal fees for settling the matter were over four million. By 1907, however, he was in the midst of a comeback, and though in a decade he would be totally destitute, Fairbanks had good reason to be pleased with his match. Right, little Beth in the days when Dad was indeed King of his particular jungle. Opposite, the young mother cradles Douglas Fairbanks, Jr., who was born December 9, 1909, in New York.

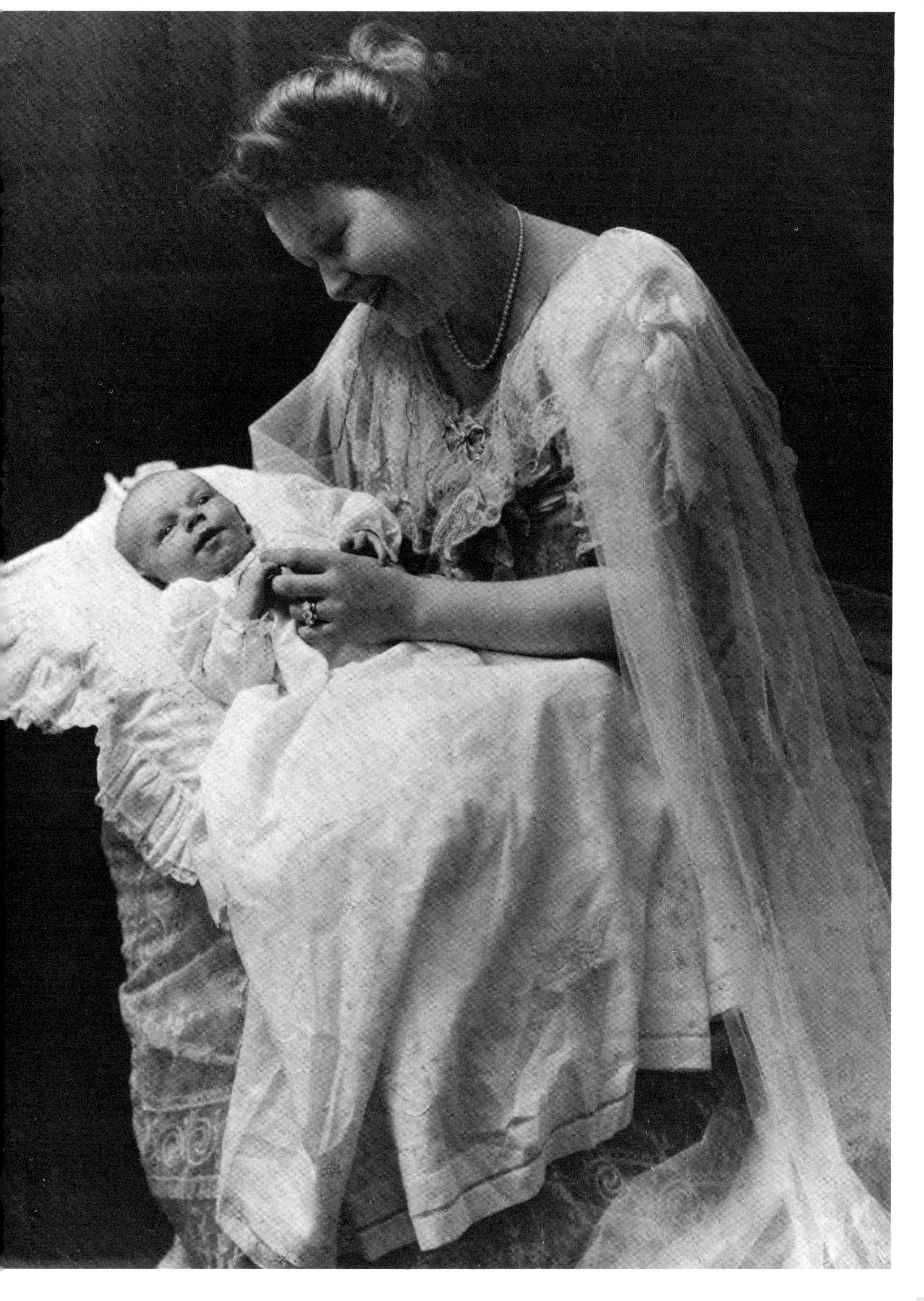

"The old world in its sunset was fair to see," Winston Churchill once wrote, and in Douglas, Jr.'s first summer—1910—the family basked in that dying glow. They rented a spacious, but not pretentious, house at Bourne End in England that was obviously well equipped from the sportsman's point of view—a dubious virtue judging from young Douglas's expression (opposite, lower right). On these pages, two historic pictures. Left, the earliest photographic evidence of Fairbanks' obsessive interest in world-class celebrities of the sort he would soon become—a snapshot he took of Ellen Terry and her husband, James Carew, on a visit to their home. Opposite, he hoists an unidentified tennis partner to his shoulders—the first of literally hundreds of such stunts he performed for the camera's benefit.

At the age of one, a set of Chinese boxes held Douglas, Jr.'s interest but presented no insoluble problems (opposite). Above, the elder Fairbanks strikes a pose for the portraitist—and almost manages a ferocity to match that of his companion. His two-year-old son, in a slightly earlier shot, opts for a more manageable beast—and demonstrates the refinement of features the Sully line contributed to the Fairbanks heritage.

Plus fours at minus four: Doug, Jr., on a Watch Hill vacation, shows a precocious interest in the game that would, in later life, become an obsession with his father. Opposite, Dad essays a moodily romantic pose—and reveals a little-known fact about himself: the man who was to become the nation's most famous exemplar of physical fitness was a heavy—almost a chain—smoker.

Apeda
N-Y

The Modern Musketeer

In the mid-teens Adolph Zukor, on his way to creating the mighty Paramount Pictures empire, also created a vogue for—as his slogan put it—"famous players in famous plays." Harry Aitkin, a shrewd, under-capitalized and now nearly forgotten would-be mogul, decided to follow Zukor's example and lured Fairbanks, among dozens of others, westward—under a $2000-per-week contract with his Triangle Studios. There the big legit starts mixed uneasily with youngsters whose prime allegiance was to the movie medium in general, to their discoverer and mentor D. W. Griffith in particular. The great director's first long masterpiece, the precedent-shattering *Birth of A Nation,* had been financed by Aitkin. Below, a few of the Triangle players gather for a portrait. Top: Dorothy Gish, Seena Owen, Norma Talmadge; center: Robert Harron, Aitkin himself, Sir Herbert Beerbohm-Tree (the original Prof. Higgins in *Pygmalion* and Aitkin's largest prize), Owen Moore (Mary Pickford's first husband), Wilfred Lucas; bottom: Fairbanks, Bessie Love, Constance Talmadge, Constance Collier, Lillian Gish, Fay Lincoln, DeWolf Hopper.

Exuberant Doug Fairbanks was a puzzlement to the sober Griffith (seen directing Lillian Gish, top). He just didn't fit into the sort of melodramas D. W. wanted to make. Young Anita Loos (center) found him a kindred spirit, a man who could carry off the kind of cheeky gags she loved but Griffith somehow never got around to filming. Why, Doug could even make granitic William S. Hart laugh (bottom).

Doug, Sr. introduces Doug, Jr. to some of his co-workers. Movie cowboys, in those days (the picture was taken in 1915), were recruited from the ranks of real-life range-riders, and the younger Fairbanks remembers being impressed by the fact that those were not costumes the riders were wearing and by the information that you could tell which western state a man hailed from by the way he creased his hat. The mighty set looming in the background is the great Walls of Babylon, the edifice Griffith had created for *Intolerance*. At right, Senior's Indian costume for *The Half Breed*. His wife objected to its immodesty and would have preferred something more along the lines of his son's get-up (below).

Debut: Or *The Lamb* (1915) turns tiger, capable of rescuing self and distressed damsel from a whole tribe of rampaging Yaquis. This first film set the pattern for the majority of Doug's early comedies, with the protagonist starting out a study in ineptitude, then, under the impress of necessity, discovering within himself an unsuspected heroic (and pragmatic) side. The unpretentiously stated message—that there is extraordinary stuff in ordinary people if only they will let it out—was cheering to a nation unconsciously mourning the frontier's passing, concerned that its virtues had gone with it.

The Lamb was an instant success, and in the three years after its release (1916–18) Douglas Fairbanks made 23 pictures, over half his lifetime's output. With his preternatural energies pouring into the process of converting himself from his old status as reliable leading man into the new one of superstar, there was little left over for wife and son, and their pensive pose (above) suggests they turned to one another for comfort. Doug, Sr., of course, loved his native west, not merely because it provided a suitably spacious backdrop for his adventures, but because its wide horizons symbolized for him (and his audience) freedom from the constraints of the modern city. Never a man to hide elevated feelings, or to restrain others from joining in them, he obviously had a high old time when he went on location in canyon country. The men helping him perilously gag it up opposite are directors Allan Dwan, the stoic with a strong belt, and John Emerson, the nervous shoulder-percher.

Now, of course, everyone understands there's more to being a movie star than just appearing before the cameras. But in the beginning the magnifying effect of lens on personality came as a surprise to all concerned. Especially popular stars had, it seemed, the power to cloud men's minds. Less than two years after he came to film Doug Fairbanks began lending his name to books of uplifting philosophy aimed at the youth market. And as a patriotic American he was pleased to lend his time and name to the cause of preparedness, then to the war effort itself. The photo below is self-explanatory; Kaiser Bill is impersonated by Bull Montana—the boxer and small-parts actor who was one of the first members of Fairbanks' ever-enlarging entourage.

More publicity. Above, he takes to the air to promote a Liberty Loan drive. Right, he appears with famed driver Ralph De Palma at an auto race in support of the same cause. But the best thing about selling war bonds was the opportunity it offered to tour the nation with best pal Charlie Chaplin and best girl Mary Pickford (below), thus permitting him to discretely practice maxim he preached overleaf.

Combining Play With Work

By Douglas Fairbanks

TO MY mind health and cheerfulness are the greatest assets one can have, whatever be one's walk in life. They did more for me on the stage than any other quality, for I never pretended to be a great actor. And in the moving picture game they have proved immensely more available than any reputation I might have gained in the legitimate. To illustrate: Many moving picture "fans" came to me in Philadelphia—where I'd played lots of times in the legitimate—and asked me if I'd ever been on the stage.

My conviction is that reputation in the legitimate, unless it be so great as to obviate the necessity of certain artistic screen qualities, is not valuable to a moving picture actor. When a great actor has appeared in the plays that he has been identified with, his usefulness in the camera field, so to speak, ceases. But the "movie" star can go on impersonating rew rôles so long as new rôles are being invented for him.

With me, health was natural, and when one has health it ought to be just as natural to develop one's athletic side as it is for water to run down-hill.

Walking is a great exercise. I would rather go afoot than ride any time. When eighteen years old, I walked through Europe just for the fun of it. It was done on a bet. There were three of us. We had fifty dollars apiece and we were going to make it last for a three-months trip.

We worked our way over on a cattle ship, and got eight shillings and a return ticket for the job. Then we tramped from Liverpool to London, doing odd jobs by the way, sleeping in the open and occasionally pilfering the withal to supply the cravings of the inner man—a regular gypsy proposition. Our method of stealing grub, when at sea, we thought to be very original, but we discovered later that it was a regular old "con" game, so old and so universally practiced that it's a wonder any sea cook ever fell for it. It can be done only once, however, so it is practicable on none but the shortest voyages, such as crossing the Channel. On the way from Dover to Calais, two of the boys—we were going steerage—lured the cook away from his galley and I went in and "pinched" the plum duff, which was nothing more nor less than a big roll of pudding done up in a sack. I had to stick it down under my coat and, believe me, it was hot enough to make a mustard plaster feel like a piece of ice!

On landing in France, we walked to Rouen, where we got a job carrying lumber and water for just enough money to pay for our room. Seeing that we had to eat, and as our original store of money was likely to be depleted through idleness, we next footed it to Paris and got a job loading wooden pavement blocks on barges. The weather was very hot and we used to go stripped to the waist, but we liked the adventure of it.

Three years ago I got the *wanderlust* so bad that I couldn't stand it any longer, so I just "beat it." I took a steamer to Cuba and walked across the island from Havana to Batabano, about one hundred and twenty miles. I took a cow-puncher with me, who had chanced to come East for the first time in his life to visit relatives. In fact, he'd never been off the range before. I had known him there as a very retiring fellow, a man who never exploited his views, and while he was a very companionable, lovable chap, I'd never put him down as knowing very much except about cattle.

But when we started to walk down there in that tropical country, he opened up like a flower, if I may use a metaphor. The novelty of the sea voyage and the strange country stimulated him, loosed his tongue, and I found that he knew a lot about plants, trees, insects, in short, the fauna and flora of Cuba; and also that he was deeply read in international affairs as well as in American politics and economics.

Later, I walked all by myself across Yucatan.

About three months ago a friend and I broke away from the routine of screen business in Los Angeles and, taking a pack mule, tramped it to Hallett's Peak, then dropped down into Middle Park and crossed the Great Divide. Then, recrossing the Divide, we made our way into the Medicine Bow range in Wyoming. It was wonderful—the birds, the animals, and everything, right close to nature. Such an experience gives a man a mental and moral housecleaning.

I have always had a longing to walk from Barcelona, Spain, to Madrid. They say it's a wonderful trip, that few strangers make it, that there are many old things and customs and little communities of primitive peoples that have never been written about. You could get a thrill a minute on a trip like that!

I like the moving picture business much more than the legitimate. Apart from one's love of nature and for outdoor work, it gives you an outlet for your ingenuity. You are not repressed as you would be on the regular stage.

The managers used to be afraid of stunts on the stage until Brady rather dubiously decided to put a fight scene into "Hawthorne of the U. S. A." It went all right, but an actor can't put up as good a fight every performance of a play as he can for the movies, where he can afford to take a chance on being laid up for a while.

Booth Tarkington

Sends us this word about Douglas Fairbanks

FAIRBANKS is a faun who has been to Sunday-school He has a pagan body which yields instantly to any heathen or gypsy impulse—such as an impulse to balance a chair on its nose while hanging from the club chandelier by one of its knees—but he has a mind reliably furnished with a full set of morals and proprieties: he would be a sympathetic companion for anybody's aunt. I don't know his age; I think he hasn't any. Certainly he will never be older—unless quicksilver can get old.

Since he has gone into the movies, millions of people have been wondering why he wanted to waste his time running for the Vice-Presidency of the United States; and in vast tracts of the country Mr. Hughes lost votes because the people feared that if they elected him and his companion on the ticket, Fairbanks would seriously neglect the movies for four long years.

Few of us would care to do the things that Fairbanks likes to do. For my part, if I were fairly certain that I could sit on a fleck of soot 381 feet above the street, on the façade of a skyscraper, I wouldn't do it. In fact, most people wouldn't do it, and their judgment in the matter is praiseworthy; but the world's gayety is considerably increased because there's one man who would do it, and does do it, and *likes* to do it!

Fairbanks would do that sort of thing if he had to pay for the privilege. If the movie people had really understood him they'd never have given him a salary; they'd have charged him a fixed sum every time he risked his neck on their property. Their films would have been just as popular—and think what they might have saved! But everybody's glad they didn't think of it, because everybody likes this national bit of property, called Fairbanks, so much.

Booth Tarkington

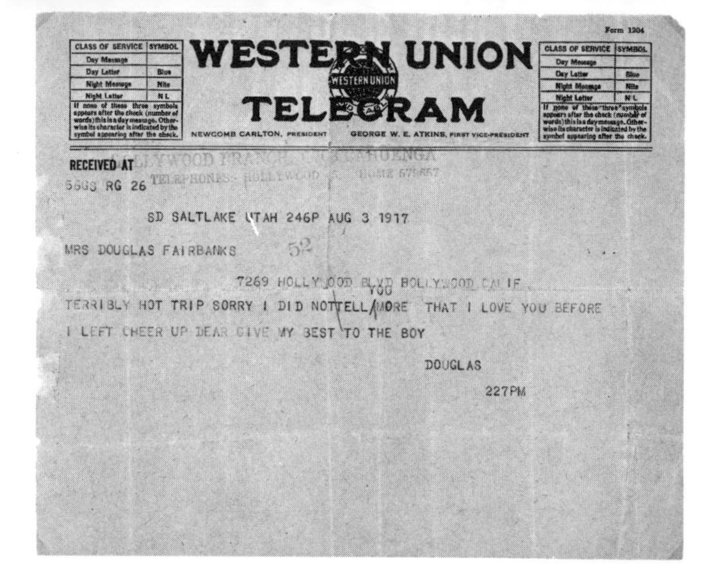

Form 1204

WESTERN UNION TELEGRAM

CLASS OF SERVICE	SYMBOL
Day Message	
Day Letter	Blue
Night Message	Nite
Night Letter	N L

If none of these three symbols appears after the check (number of words) this is a day message. Otherwise its character is indicated by the symbol appearing after the check.

NEWCOMB CARLTON, PRESIDENT GEORGE W. E. ATKINS, FIRST VICE-PRESIDENT

RECEIVED AT

5GGS RG 26

SD SALTLAKE UTAH 246P AUG 3 1917

MRS DOUGLAS FAIRBANKS 52

7269 HOLLYWOOD BLVD HOLLYWOOD CALIF

TERRIBLY HOT TRIP SORRY I DID NOTTELL YOU MORE THAT I LOVE YOU BEFORE I LEFT CHEER UP DEAR GIVE MY BEST TO THE BOY

DOUGLAS

227PM

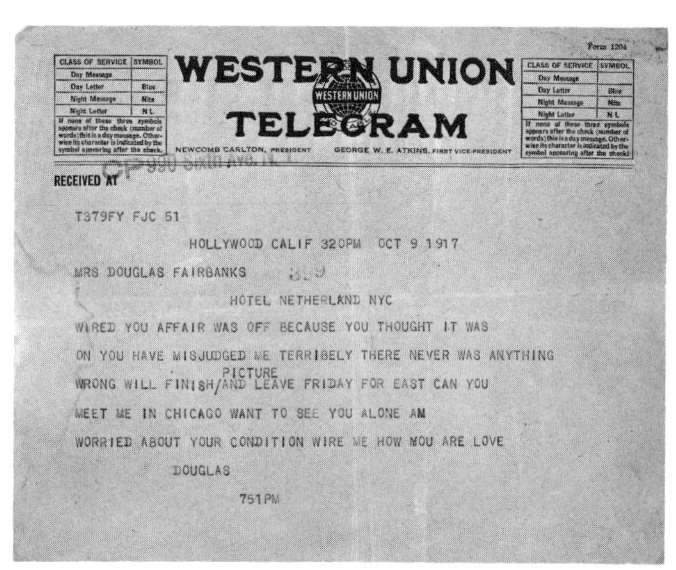

Form 1204

WESTERN UNION TELEGRAM

CLASS OF SERVICE	SYMBOL
Day Message	
Day Letter	Blue
Night Message	Nite
Night Letter	N L

If none of these three symbols appears after the check (number of words) this is a day message. Otherwise its character is indicated by the symbol appearing after the check.

NEWCOMB CARLTON, PRESIDENT GEORGE W. E. ATKINS, FIRST VICE-PRESIDENT

RECEIVED AT

T379FY FJC 51

HOLLYWOOD CALIF 320PM OCT 9 1917

MRS DOUGLAS FAIRBANKS

HOTEL NETHERLAND NYC

WIRED YOU AFFAIR WAS OFF BECAUSE YOU THOUGHT IT WAS ON YOU HAVE MISJUDGED ME TERRIBELY THERE NEVER WAS ANYTHING WRONG WILL FINISH PICTURE AND LEAVE FRIDAY FOR EAST CAN YOU MEET ME IN CHICAGO WANT TO SEE YOU ALONE AM WORRIED ABOUT YOUR CONDITION WIRE ME HOW MOU ARE LOVE

DOUGLAS

751PM

The affair between Doug and Mary probably began around 1916, and by 1917 the star was compelled to send placatory telegrams to his wife, the survival of which, over the years, seems remarkable and somehow touching. He was obviously a hard man to give up. It was probably the heady Liberty Loan tour of 1918 which finished the marriage for good. The outpouring of affection he received from the crowds equaled that given Little Mary and Chaplin, seen kneeling in foreground with Marie Dressler in the photo below commemorating tour's end. The response confirmed the idea that he was a fit consort for Mary—even to tough, shrewd Ma Pickford, who is seen to the right of her. The rising young pol at far left was told by Fairbanks that he ought really to consider a career in show business, such was one pro's judgment of FDR's charm and charisma.

The World Safe For Smiles

They Are Soldiers Of Happiness

An Old-Fashioned Vaudeville Singing Team

Now We're Off Again. The End of the Chorus of "While Strolling Through the Park One Day" Always Concluded With This Posture. A Very High Order of Talent is Required to Do This and Still Live

And This Dear Old Interpolation When One of the Artists Asks the Other a Question Fraught With Humor, and When the Other Replies the First Smites Him in the Countenance With a Folded Newspaper

This is My Page and I Insist Upon Giving My Well-Known Impersonation of Napoleon Before We Proceed With Our Performance as Planned

And Then the Partners in Those Dear Old Teams, After Singing "While Strolling Through the Park One Day" Across the Country and Back, Would Return to This, the Art of Their Youth, Wherein They Excelled All Others

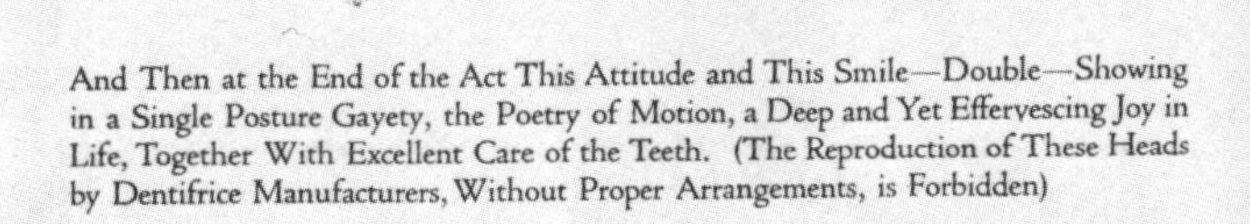

And Then at the End of the Act This Attitude and This Smile—Double—Showing in a Single Posture Gayety, the Poetry of Motion, a Deep and Yet Effervescing Joy in Life, Together With Excellent Care of the Teeth. (The Reproduction of These Heads by Dentifrice Manufacturers, Without Proper Arrangements, is Forbidden)

And Even We, in All Probability, Should Have Had to Revert to the Shining Profession Illustrated Above, Had Not a Humanitarian Inventor Perfected the Moving-Picture Machine, Rendering Possible Our Embalmment, So to Speak, in Celluloid, for Generations Yet Unborn. On Behalf of My Imitative Associate and Myself, I Thank You

(Signed) *Charlie Chaplin*
(Approved) *Douglas Fairbanks*

Photographs by Charles Warrington and William Finn

Douglas and Beth Fairbanks separated in the spring of 1918, his pals gave the evidence required for a New York divorce, and a month before the matter was finally settled in court Douglas, Jr. received the consolation prize of this curious White House postcard. He associated his father with "a pleasant, energetic, and agreeable 'atmosphere' about the house, to which I was somehow attached, but which was not attached to me. He also seemed to be someone I did not know very well." And, one must say, vice versa. Still, the Dear Boy was not a complainer and for a time he soldiered bravely on as a member of New York's fashionable Knickerbocker Greys. Unfortunately, his mother's generous divorce settlement would be diminished by unwise investments and he would suffer hard times economically as well as psychologically in the years to come. Meanwhile, his father fretted that he would become a Mama's Boy in the exclusive care of this woman he described as a "dominating, possessive and extravagant character," who was also, in her son's words, "very loving, sympathetic and generous-hearted." Dad, unfortunately, did not choose to do anything very practical to allay his concerns.

WIFE DIVORCES FAIRBANKS OF SCREEN FAME

NOV 30 1918

Interlocutory Decree Granted on Evidence of "Beautiful Girl" Party Given by Movie Star

Actor Denies Charges, but Fails to Defend Case in Court, and Wife Gets Custody of Only Son

Dec. 1, 1918

Mrs. Douglas Fairbanks, wife of the screen star, won an interlocutory decree of divorce in White Plains yesterday. The corespondent was referred to in the testimony and documents as "an unknown woman," with whom the actor was intimate "in a house on Thirty-third street."

Mrs. Fairbanks, the plaintiff, was awarded the custody of their eight-year-old child, Douglas, Jr. No alimony was mentioned in the interlocutory decree handed down by Supreme Court Justice J. Addison Young, but it is understood that a large allowance was settled on the wife. Mrs. Fairbanks said her husband earned more than $10,000 a week. Neither party in the action can remarry until six months from to-day, when the divorce may be made final.

William Clifton Crawford, vaudeville comedian, and John Emerson, moving picture director, were the chief witnesses for Mrs. Fairbanks, and theirs was the only testimony read into the record. Both are former friends of the screen star, who filed a general denial to his wife's charges, but did not contest the suit in court.

ACTORS TELLS OF PARTY.

Mr. Crawford testified that on January 3, 1916, he met Fairbanks at the Lambs Gambol, and the latter invited him to "a party in the Thirty-third street house where there were beautiful girls." After they entered the house, Crawford said he saw Fairbanks and a young woman smoking cigarettes in a bedroom in negligee.

John Emerson's testimony was that at Hollywood, California, in January, 1918, Fairbanks told him of this party, adding it was the best time he ever had in his life.

Mrs. Fairbanks is living with her son in New Rochelle. She is a daughter of Daniel Sully, the erstwhile cotton king.

The Fairbankses were married at Watch Hill, Rhode Island, on July 7, 1907. Marital trouble between the film favorite and his pretty wife first became known to the public last April, when Mrs. Fairbanks announced they were living apart.

WERE BEST OF FRIENDS.

She said they were the best of friends, that her husband was the kindest and most considerate of men, but that their paths lay apart. Mrs. Fairbanks insisted there would be no divorce, because there were no grounds for such action.

She referred to a moving picture star contemptuously, expressing regret that this woman's name should have been linked with that of her husband. Mrs. Fairbanks explained this intimacy was no concern of hers, but she was tired of defending him. For the sake of their boy, she said, she had to put an end to gossip by announcing their separation.

When Fairbanks read that statement he denied the slightest friction existed in his family. The printed reports, he asserted, were pro-German propaganda, designed to interfere with his work in the Liberty Loan drive.

When seen at the Algonquin [illegible] where she was lunching yesterday, Mrs. Fairbanks was radiant. She was dressed in the most becoming costume imaginable, with a saucy little hat covered with pink roses, not near so prettily pink as her cheeks.

"Happy?" she returned the question put to her after she had learned of the outcome of her divorce case.

"Don't I look happy? Everybody is happy to-day. I haven't been living in New York. I was up in the country. But I just had to run into town to-day.

"I don't want to talk about this thing. I honestly haven't a thing left to say. I've said such an awful lot already."

And with that she laughed infectiously and suggested there wasn't a scheme or a plan in her head or heart that she wanted to cover up.

As for maidens who have a weakness for celebrities—she wouldn't discuss the pros nor cons of such mating.

"Well, you see me," she averred. And certainly she appeared very lovely.

Her young son, Douglas, Jr., came into the city with her. She adores him, and she says his father does, too. She is glad of that and doesn't want any estrangement of their affections.

ALIMONY KEPT SECRET.

Mrs. Fairbanks' lawyer, M. Mahlstat, of New Rochelle, said last night he was pleased over his client's victory. He said Mr. Fairbanks was out West and he did not know when the two had met last. He is not sure whether the movie star saw his wife and little boy when in New York for the Liberty Loan or not. It is understood, though, that the little family met and the father and son had a rollicking good time together. He said:

"The matter of alimony did not come before the court. Alimony was asked when the suit was filed but a satisfactory agreement was made between Mr. and Mrs. Fairbanks. I am not at liberty to tell just how much she will receive."

Throughout the divorce proceedings, Mrs. Fairbanks showed no bitterness toward her husband. She said simply that they would all be happier with a separation and that she really wanted her husband to live his life as it would give him most pleasure. She expressed the kindest regard for him.

Yesterday, she intimated that her feeling toward her divorced husband had not altered since she made those expressions.

Wanderings: Beth Fairbanks rebounded into a brief, unhappy marriage to stockbroker James Evans, lost much of her $400,000 divorce settlement by trying to increase it through speculation. She and her son—whose chubbiness and lack of academic aptitude were a source of pain to his father at this time—drifted back to Los Angeles, where, among other schools, Douglas attended Harvard Military Academy, an expensive file drawer for the sons of *haut* Hollywood. The youngster, obviously, was able to keep a cheerful face on things and by 1921—even allowing for a fashionable portraitist's idealizations (opposite), it is clear that he had outgrown the awkward age. About that time, mother and son removed to Paris for the same reason the writers of the Lost Generation did—to stretch thin resources further by virtue of the favorable exchange rate. "Every so often mother would pop a jewel so we could keep going," Douglas, Jr. now recalls, not at all unhappily.

Out of sight, out of mind—that was Doug's attitude toward his late family. In 1919, as the flow of production and publicity continued unabated, he was preoccupied by the creation of a new business family—United Artists. At an informal meeting of the founders (above) D. W. Griffith wears one of his characteristically splendid hats and Charlie's finger expresses their collective attitude toward the Hollywood establishment, which did not believe artists, united or not, could manage the complexities of show-biz business.

WOMAN'S HOME COMPANION PICTURE SECTION FOR JULY, 1919

The One and Only "Doug" Himself

Idol of countless movie fans, who thrill with delight as he leaps on and off express trains, swings from perilous heights, and finds new ways to defy gravitation in every film. An article by Doug, describing the most dangerous and daring of his stunts and giving some of his views of life, will be found on page 24

"ALL very well, young man," said Madame Nellie Melba, the great singer; "but you'd better take care and not be *too* daring!" "Believe me, dear lady," replied Doug, "I'm the most careful little fellow you ever saw in your life." And then he went out and walked all about the yard on the top of a tall ladder, as you behold him at the right, a feat to make the rest of us mortals shudder.

THE most dangerous stunt he ever did—jumping the Grand Canyon. He says of this feat: "Never again!"

WHEN Fred Stone is around, he and Doug are always stumping each other to feats of agility and acrobatics. Just above you may behold them leaping over a bar, in graceful flying attitudes—just like dear little angels, as one of their admirers quaintly remarked. We don't say they are *not* angelic creatures, either of them, but we sha'n't be led on to say they *are*, either.

AT THE right, ladies and gentlemen, you behold Doug and his famous laughing horse—the only animal of its kind in captivity. This horse laughs because he enjoys so much playing in the movies with Doug, and Doug laughs because it's so funny to see a horse laugh a real horse-laugh. And there we are, everybody happy.

His Majesty the star as *His Majesty the American* (1919). In this year, he was ranked as the nation's number one male box office attraction, and despite repeated denials all around, it seemed unimaginable that he would not shortly marry the screen's number one female favorite. Meantime, this first United Artists release was—delightfully—not greatly different from his previous films. Once again he was, as an earlier subtitle had it, "an all-around chap, just a regular American," though here, as another subtitle said (and these stills prove) he was "an excitement-hunting thrill-hound," bored with the proprieties of city life—as many young men in his audience were. Fairbanks himself was such an obviously good-natured sort that he could in this and other comedies of the time satirize everything from success literature to pop psychology without offending even the true believers in these fads. He could, it seemed, do just about anything he wanted, on screen or off, without risking loss of his audience. And there were, indeed, some things he wanted very badly.

More nonsense from *His Majesty the American.* Fairbanks' more spectacular acrobatics make such arresting photos that film historians have tended to neglect the purely goony aspects of his comic work. But the innocent merriment of scenes like these prove the truth of a contemporary critical assertion that "Douglas Fairbanks is a tonic. He laughs and you feel relieved." He accepted—and no one objected to—billing as "the best-liked figure on the screen." In picture at right Frank Campeau, longtime Fairbanks friend and foil, leads the feckless pursuit of the modern Ariel.

NON
SI
NE

At one point while making *His Majesty,* Doug and Co. (which included director Victor Fleming, later to make *The Wizard of Oz* and *Gone With the Wind*) land in the drink (below). He had no intention of allowing this production still to become a symbol of his life, and he laid desperate siege to Mary Pickford, at last persuading her to head for Reno and divorce from Owen Moore. While she was thus occupied he found himself up a tree—with the waters rising—in a satire he called optimistically, and appropriately, as it turned out, *When the Clouds Roll By.* In a matter of months, they would.

Another transition—from effete Eastern playboy (below) to dashing democratic hero, in *The Mollycoddle.* Another awesome leap—into the arms of a waiting stuntman, athletic high point of that 1920 picture. Transitions and leaps were, if anything, more than ever on Doug's mind that spring. For on March 28 there occurred a solemn, simple ceremony that a French writer of the time could not resist terming a "poetic and audacious" act—Hollywood's first royal wedding, the marriage of Douglas Elton Ulman and little Gladys Smith, to call Doug and Mary by their rightful names for the last time before their permanent symbiotic joining on the world's tongue as beloved, perfectly matched Doug-and-Mary.

"The marriage was the logical end of the Fairbanks role as popular philosopher," Alistair Cooke would write. "He could do no more. He who had preached in many a short sentence and many a rocketing leap across the screen that rewards can be won in this world, had won the hand of the girl so fragile and winsome that every man wanted her—for a sister. Douglas Fairbanks and Mary Pickford came to mean more than a couple of married film stars. They were a living proof of America's chronic belief in happy endings." Yet the event itself was deliberately understated; they were married in the minister's study, they celebrated with a quiet dinner at Pickfair—the great house Fairbanks had begun building in Beverly Hills when this marriage must have seemed no more than a delightfully ambitious fantasy. The guest list was composed entirely of family and close friends, who foregathered under the porte cochere for this formal record of a historic event. From left: Charles Chaplin, Edward Knoblock (playwright and soon-to-be screenwriter), Marjorie Daw (actress and sometime great and good friend of the groom), brother Robert Fairbanks, Jack Pickford, Charlotte Pickford (the ultimate stage mother), the bridal pair, Mrs. Robert Fairbanks, and Benny Ziedman, pal and inevitable press agent.

Doug and Mary

If the wedding was quiet, the wedding trip—three months later—was anything but. It started out routinely enough: Doug stunting for the cameramen perilously close to roof's edge at New York's Ritz-Carlton; the royal couple making a democratic call on their hotel's below-stairs staff; then posing amiably for ship's photographers aboard their unromantically named barque, the S.S. *Lapland.* But . . .

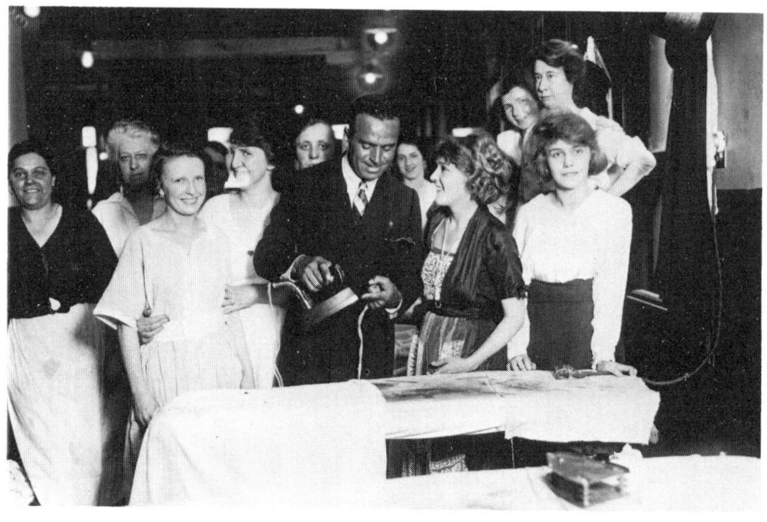

. . . when they reached the other side, expectant boat train smiles soon gave way to panic. Almost every time they stepped outside they were mobbed—as at Christiania (Oslo) (above right), and Paris (below). The movies—inexpensive, universally available, offering magnified, romantic images of their stars—invested them with historically unprecedented magic; simple folks would risk anything (including injury) to be literally in touch with it. A wire service caption accompanying one of these photos called it "an example of freak lure" and suggested darkly that since wherever stars appear crowds gather, "something's going to happen." That "something" very nearly did occur in civilized England at a charity fête.

JARDIN des PLANTES
COMPAGNIE

The face of fear. The site was London's normally peaceful Kensington Gardens, the occasion a combined bazaar and lawn party, where no one expected the crush Doug, Mary, and other theatrical stars would generate. The terror began with a shouted request to shake hands, to which Pickford unthinkingly responded. She was grabbed by others seeking the same favor and her husband had to clutch her by the ankles to prevent her being yanked from the car. Later, on foot, seeking sanctuary and an anonymous escape vehicle, he hoisted her to his shoulders (for the first of many times in their life together).

None the worse for wear. Or so the photo of their arrival home on the S.S. *Olympic* seems to indicate. The comically bland trade-paper items indicate a studied attempt by the stars to play the role of good sports. After all, their audience was international and there was no reason to offend anyone. Indeed, their feelings about the whole experience were ambivalent. They did manage a few quiet days in Wiesbaden—and actually discovered that they missed, if not the crowds, then their adoration. Still, Mary never really learned to love travel as her husband did—and this difference in taste was to become an issue in their marriage. Perhaps the most significant event of their trip, however, was a piece of reading Mary did—a story that had been submitted to her husband. Based on her enthusiasm, he cabled orders home to begin building sets and sewing costumes—without bothering to read it. When he did, he must have sensed that it offered a unique opportunity to turn his career in a new direction without completely sacrificing the identity he had established with his public. The name of the property was *The Mark of Zorro*, and he is seen, overleaf, as the mysterious yet benign outlaw of California in the days when it was ruled by Spain.

1002 THE MOVING PICTURE WORLD

First-Hand Story of Ovation Tendered to Douglas and Mary by Paris Crowds

By our Special Correspondent

Paris, July 20.

DOUGLAS FAIRBANKS AND MARY PICKFORD are here, and have taken Paris by storm. They are stopping at the Hotel de Crillon (known to Americans as the United States Army headquarters during the war), having recently arrived from Italy, Switzerland and Austria, which they visited at a speed that to the Frenchman is "the lightning fashion of the American." Mary explained that Venice had always been one of the cities of her dreams and that the reality had not been disappointing. She and her husband motored on to Milan. They came to Paris by train from Geneva.

The pair speak a little French. I heard the "world's sweetheart" making a creditable attempt at a conversation with a French journalist, but it was obviously a relief to her when she was interrupted by a call from her husband.

Their names are pronounced in the French manner, Mary becomes "Marie" and Fairbanks is familiarly "Doug," pronounced "Doog." However, Doug's announcement that he intended to appear later in a made-in-France version of "The Three Musketeers," has caused him to be dubbed D'Artagnan.

To Make Picture in France.

Something of the interest that England is still taking in the pair is shown by the fact that the photographer from the London "Sketch," who was waiting their arrival in Paris, left at once by special aeroplane for London after securing a photograph of the two in the Place de la Concorde.

Mary told me she and her husband would return to France in October, and she called upon him to confirm her statement. "My wife's plans for a French picture are still uncompleted," he said, "but I shall start work here in the autumn on 'The Three Musketeers' with a cast partly French and partly American. I have been studying the story and see wonderful possibilities in it."

Both are enthusiastic about the possibilities that lie in the continental scenery for moving picture work, and both hold to the belief that in the near future American stars will be continually and often crossing the water to make pictures on this side.

Visited American Battle Line.

The two went up to the battle front on Sunday to visit a portion of the old American line. Monday they were entertained at luncheon at the Pavillon des Champs Elysées by the directorate of Comoedia, the well-known theatrical daily. The guests included Messrs. de Baroncelli, editor of the Film d'Art, Leon Brezillon, president of the Association of Managers of Moving Picture Theatres; Rene de Prejelan, the well-known artist; Gaston Fleury and Herve Lauwick, of "Figaro"; Verhylle of "L'Ecran"; Mme. Betty and Mons. de Max of the Theatre Comedie Francaise; Mme. Devesme, editor of the Cine Globe; Mme. Jasmine, the danseuse; Mons. Raymond Gaumont and Mons. E. Costil, representing the Gaumont interests; Tor de Arozarena of "The Stage," and very many others.

George Casella, editor-in-chief of Comoedia, did the honors of the banquet and proposed the toast to the two American guests.

Made Speeches in French.

Both the guests made short speeches in French, "Doog" even improvising a bit in the foreign language. He loved everything in Paris, he declared—its streets, its buildings, its distances, "but the real beauty of Paris, it is its women!" While coffee was being served upon the terrace afterwards photographers from all Paris' dailies and weeklies buzzed about like flies. A matinee had been staged that afternoon at the Salle d'Olympia for the benefit of the two. Their arrival in the theatre was the signal for a tremendous ovation on the part of the audience.

Mary and Doug Find Europe Poor Spot for a 'Quiet Honeymoon'

BY MILTON BRONNER

LONDON, July 2—"Hello America! Gee, we're having a fine time here, but we'll be glad to get back, too, for a rest!"

That's Douglas Fairbanks' honeymoon message to the folks back home.

Doug and his bride, Mary Pickford, are receiving a reception such as they never dreamed of. The crowds are tremendous—larger and more enthusiastic than any that greeted the newlyweds at home.

Douglas is sorry he won't be home on Fourth of July, "when the rockets sizz and the crackers biff-bang."

"But here they have things sizz, too—in a glass," said Mary.

No Corner on Back-Slapping

Doug smiled and continued:

"And speaking of biff-banging, I've been biff-banged on the back day after day by the friendly Britishers until—say! I thought slapping people on the back was an American custom 'all rights reserved.'

"At first when I saw the 'entire British nation' advancing I wondered what was up. It soon developed that the advance was friendly. All they wanted was to kiss Mary. I had to tell 'em that's my job.

"In the language of the west. I thought we would only hit the high spots of Europe and have a quiet honeymoon, but Gosh, we are chinning the moon! I can't see the buildings for the people.

"And 'quiet honeymoon'"—! z! !

British Sports and Good Folks

"It's nice to be in a foreign land where they speak our tongue and say nice things about America in language we can read. The British are good sports and good folks.

"I think there ought to be a gypsy curse on any one who tries to get up a scrap between us."

Mary laughed.

"You're a bum preacher, Doug," said she. "But I want to put a postscript on your talk to America—

"To all you Americans who have been so good to me I send love. And sign it 'From one who is just a wee tiny bit homesick!'"

DF-19

By day, Zorro was a hopeless fop and idler, the despair of his powerful father; by night, he was the tireless defender of threatened virtue. At all times Fairbanks fascinated the wildly popular physical culture magazines of his day (opposite).

Analyzing Douglas Fairbanks

By Carl Easton Williams

THE mystery of Douglas Fairbanks. For some years now the entire world has contemplated that mystery—how "Doug" does it.

We have seen him make all kinds of more or less impossible jumps; sometimes up, sometimes down, sometimes from roof to roof. We have seen him climb walls and porches and bridges and other seemingly inaccessible places. We have seen him dive over fences and through windows in the apparently most reckless and devil-may-care fashion. We have seen him fight whole bunches of villains, sometimes empty-handed, sometimes with swords—never with custard pies. And we have wondered how he did it. So let's look him over. What is Douglas Fairbanks, anyway? He is, first of all, a personality — one of the two or three most unique personalities on the screen. He is an exponent of whimsical comedy. He is, indeed, the embodied spirit of refined comedy, with the distinction that his is a special brand of the same—light comedy with a dash that represents the spirit of American youth, and then some.

Then, also, he is our most versatile stunt performer, and while we revel in his comedy, just as we delight in that of Mary Pickford, Dorothy Gish or Taylor Holmes, we also marvel at his stunts. At first glimpse these stunts seem purely athletic in character. But the truth is that this same spirit of dashing, whimsical comedy is a big factor even in the performance of those stunts. For the thing that we call Fairbanks, the thing that makes "Doug" what he is, is both muscular and mental. The things he does, athletically and acrobatically, are not merely a matter of strength and speed, but of spirit. They are an expres-

Showing both what he can do and why he is able to do it. This is the Fairbanks physique in action—very much in action. "Doug" jumped five feet into the air for this picture, which was taken expressly for PHYSICAL CULTURE.

Fairbanks was not entirely blithe about doing costume drama, and in case the public found him unacceptable with unfamiliar sword in hand, he offered them a choice—a contemporary comedy based on the models that had succeeded so well in the past. But *The Nut,* despite some obviously fine, silly stuff (left), was one of his few failures. Along with other producers, he was discovering that there was a huge market for action-filled drama set in a past remote enough so that it could be romanticized—and not remind people of the tragic slaughter the world had just witnessed in the trenches of France. About the efficacy of gag photos Fairbanks never had any doubt, and they flowed from his studio in an endless stream. Opposite, he and Chaplin ape terror as heavyweight champ Jack Dempsey apes ferocity.

Doug—with a little help from Mary—taught Hollywood the joys of cosmopolitanism. One week Mary's brother, Jack Pickford, might turn out to help entertain the Duchess de Gramont (left); the next, Bill Tilden and Manuel Alonzo might join Doug and Chaplin for some spirited doubles.

Doug was, of course, an apostle of fitness and had a fully equipped gym at his studio. In the study below he shows his smooth form a few years later as he masters a new skill—throwing the *bola,* a kind of Argentinian lasso, for *The Gaucho.*

And then, of course, there was Pickfair—so named by the press, not its owners. Unlike so many of the houses that are its peers in popular lore, it was not designed to inspire awe but to be lived in comfortably. Rambling casually over its hilltop site, it was—and is—tastefully but not oppressively furnished. And though the Fairbankses were capable of putting on a grand evening for a visiting dignitary, their idea of a really good time was to invite a few close friends in to see a new movie in the living room, where they noshed peanut brittle and the master often dozed off before the film had run its full course. The statue in the postcard below has been moved, and much remodeling and redecoration has taken place over the 55 years Mary Pickford has remained in residence.

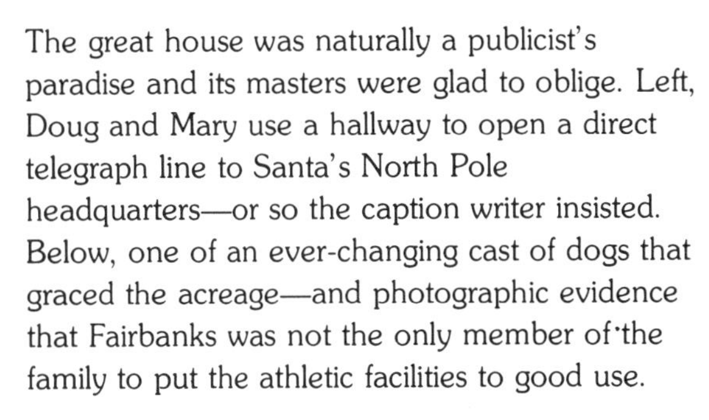

The great house was naturally a publicist's paradise and its masters were glad to oblige. Left, Doug and Mary use a hallway to open a direct telegraph line to Santa's North Pole headquarters—or so the caption writer insisted. Below, one of an ever-changing cast of dogs that graced the acreage—and photographic evidence that Fairbanks was not the only member of the family to put the athletic facilities to good use.

Pickfair top to bottom. Doug's surprisingly austere bedroom; the main hall and the living room, both graced by the western paintings (most by Remington or Charles Russell) for which Fairbanks had a true passion; the dining room, which has latterly been greatly improved by a lighter décor.

Canoe runs were a popular feature among Hollywood homemakers in the twenties and Pickfair had one. Below, playwright Knoblock tries to get a little work done—no easy matter when star—and photographer—were present.

Director Fred Niblo joins Knoblock and Fairbanks in a one-for-all, all-for-one pose on the set of *The Three Musketeers.*

The Musketeers and friend: Leon Barry was Athos, George Siegmann was Porthos, Eugene Palette, Aramis.

The Three Musketeers was a story Fairbanks had loved since childhood and it was by far the grandest production he had ever attempted on screen. Opposite, his famous entrance on a plug farm horse. Right, practice makes perfect the most famous bit of acrobatics in the film—his one-hand handspring (with sword).

Robert E. Sherwood—a friend of Fairbanks and a movie critic before he became a playwright and advisor to presidents—summed up the appeal of the movie neatly: "When Alexandre Dumas sat down at his desk, smoothed his hair back, chewed the end of his quill pen and said to himself, 'Well, I guess I might as well write a book called *The Three Musketeers,*' he doubtless had but one object in view: to provide a suitable story for Douglas Fairbanks to act in the movies." Ambitious as it was, however, there was always time for a gag shot. Above, Pickford hitches a ride on D'Artagnan's plug.

A child—in this case Dick Winslow, the son of family friends—could nearly always charm Douglas Fairbanks into naturalness (opposite), something his wife (below) could rarely manage when a camera was present. Visiting celebrities (like Somerset Maugham in the group above left) or pals (like Chaplin, below left) inevitably brought out the show-off. One must imagine, of course, that in those busy days when his marriage, his career, his style of life were among the most envied in America, the depressive side of Fairbanks' mildly manic-depressive personality was not much in evidence. It would have its innings, its revenge, later.

Hardly a week goes by that Charlie doesn't drop over to the studio to see Doug and Mary and when he does there is always something doing. Mary, you will ..., is wearing a quite grown-up costume as "Rosita."

Poor little poor boy. Douglas, Jr. was also in Europe that summer, touring the battlefields (above, he and a French lad pose with Big Bertha), preparing to settle down there. Father and son did not meet.

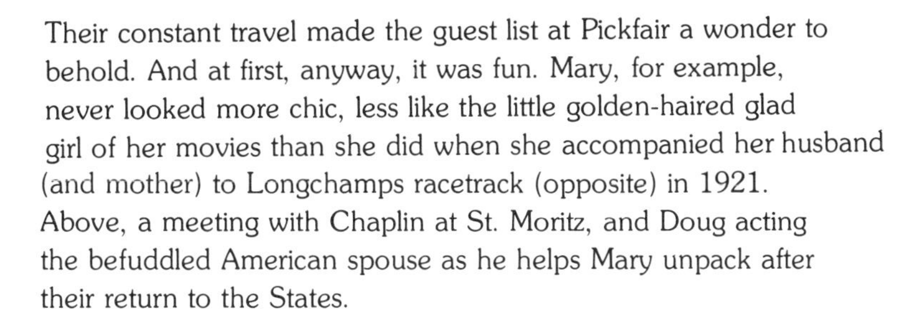

Their constant travel made the guest list at Pickfair a wonder to behold. And at first, anyway, it was fun. Mary, for example, never looked more chic, less like the little golden-haired glad girl of her movies than she did when she accompanied her husband (and mother) to Longchamps racetrack (opposite) in 1921. Above, a meeting with Chaplin at St. Moritz, and Doug acting the befuddled American spouse as he helps Mary unpack after their return to the States.

Immediately after their vacation, the great battlements of the *Robin Hood* sets began to challenge the Hollywood skies. They rivaled the ones Griffith had flung up for *Intolerance,* and in all the years since no one has surpassed these great conceits of these great showmen—perhaps because something like the spirit of the artist also moved in both of them. Fairbanks, however, was too much the regular guy, too much embued with the dominant business ethic of the twenties to admit artistic leanings. And he did, quite genuinely, love to set mighty enterprises in train, to be a mover and shaker, an industrial leader. His quick, rough art suffered from this ambition. "Where once he danced on air, Doug now stands on ceremony," a critic wrote of his spectacular period. The judgment is too harsh; some of the ceremonies (overleaf) were, remain, without peer.

The colossal sets for *Robin Hood* were Fairbanks' idea, but when he first saw the astounding castle built by art director Wilfred Buckland he was not only awed but dismayed. "I can't compete with that," he told director Allan Dwan. But in fact he found inspired ways to use the gigantic scale. Right, he escapes up the steps of a tower, emerges on the balcony at right and — cornered—swoops down the huge drape that trails to the floor—with the help of a child's slide hidden in its folds. (Dwan's idea, but Fairbanks knew a good one when he heard it.) As for reaching the impossibly high windows, he simply swung in on a vine.

Especially in *Robin Hood's* second half, when the hero was forced into outlawry, the old Doug was very much in evidence, not in the least buried under period splendor. In this leap (opposite) he demonstrated what Alistair Cooke called his "glory, the mystery of his visual fascination," which was that he could throw all the textbook tricks of the gymnast "on the makeshift apparatus of ordinary life." Above, Doug permitted his wife to borrow Allan Dwan's megaphone for a publicity picture and (below) gave athlete Jim Thorpe a lesson in the art of the broadsword for the same purposes.

When one spectacle is finished, another inevitably begins—the spectacle of publicity. Sid Grauman, famous for his Chinese Theater in Hollywood, and a relentless friend to many stars, contributed lyrics to the theme music that all major productions provided the orchestras accompanying silent pictures in their first runs; then he oversaw the business of recording the handprints and autographs of star and wife in a cement square in the forecourt of his theater.

He shot an arrow into the air—and he wasn't supposed to. It was good enough for the photographers, when Doug arrived in New York to hype *Robin Hood,* if he just gave a realistic tug on the bowstring. But as Allan Dwan has said, "some deviltry within him" made him loose the arrow—and it lodged in the backside of a tailor who had made the mistake of leaving a window open when Fairbanks was in town. The missile's two-block run was impressive and so was the $5000 the star settled on his startled victim. Made the publicity all the more potent, and a day later he cheerfully permitted his bride to powder him down in public. Virile fellow—never the slightest question about that.

UNITING STAGE AND MOVIE LAND: A GLITTERING ARRAY OF THEATRICAL PERSONAGES AT THE WEDDING OF MARILYNN MILLER AND JACK PICKFORD.
In the First Row Are: Douglas Fairbanks, Mary Pickford, the Bride, the Bridegroom and "Ma" Pickford, With Charlie Chaplin Displaying His Best Off-Stage Smile, a Scene Registered Immediately After the Ceremony at Los Angeles, Cal. (International.)

Jack Pickford's wedding to musical comedy star Marilynn Miller (opposite, above) had a royal quality about it almost as potent as that surrounding Doug and Mary's earlier marriage. But Jack was a tragic figure, driven to alcohol and dope by trying to make an acting career in big sister's shadow and he would die young and near madness. Critic Robert Sherwood's match (below) would prove more lasting. John Emerson and his wife, Anita Loos, are the other couple joining Doug and Mary in the wedding party. Sherwood was already dreaming of success as playwright, probably could not imagine his later role as presidential advisor and biographer. Beth Sully (right), divorced a second time, but somehow never prettier, looked on from a distant obscurity, some time away still from her last, happy marriage to Jack Whiting, the popular singer.

The studio turned out a Boy Scout honor guard to welcome Douglas, Jr. to Hollywood after he signed his first movie contract, and publicity (opposite) stressed the road he had traveled from brief boyhood chubbiness to adolescent attractiveness. Dad was furious, believing the boy was being exploited and that the whole business was an elaborate scheme to embarrass him, which in part it was. But his mother and her family, also fallen on hard times, needed the money (this was exaggerated in press reports), and the youth was pleased to help out, pull his weight in a manly manner, though he had no special fondness at the time for the actor's life or the limelight.

Doug, Junior

Photograph by C. Smith Gardne

At seven years of age, Douglas Fairbanks, Junior, looks like a little boy you would find it pleasant to have living in your house—and not especially like a potential movie star. . . .

. . . Yet here only six years later we find him a movie star, in truth. Famous Players-Lasky have Doug, Junior, under a contract which calls for his appearance in their films at the salary of one thousand dollars a week

For the last few years, Doug has been abroad with his mother where he has enjoyed the finest schooling there is to be had. And now he will continue his lessons under a private tutor, dividing his time between his books and the Kleig lights. At first, we understand, Doug will be cast as a boy of about his own years . . . but in stories which will give him ample opportunities to display his prowess at feats, similar to those done by his famed father

Photograph by Underwood and Underwood

At the left is an old picture taken during the Liberty Loan drives when Doug toured the States with his father, selling we forget how many hundred thousand dollars' worth of Liberty Bonds. Then he shone in a reflected glory. Perhaps the near future will find him enjoying the popularity of his personal achievement

The story was by Richard Harding Davis; the director was Joseph Henabery, a competent Griffith-trained pro (he had played Abraham Lincoln in *The Birth of a Nation*). Indeed, one can imagine young Douglas identifying strongly with the character he was playing, a youth who fails a course in Turkish history, is sent by his father to that country to brush up on the subject, then proves himself worthy of the old man by rescuing the Sultan's son from bandits and winning a medal. At the time the younger Fairbanks must surely have wished that there was some such simple way to win his father's affectionate regard. Alas, the picture turned out poorly—and seemed to prove Senior's doubts.

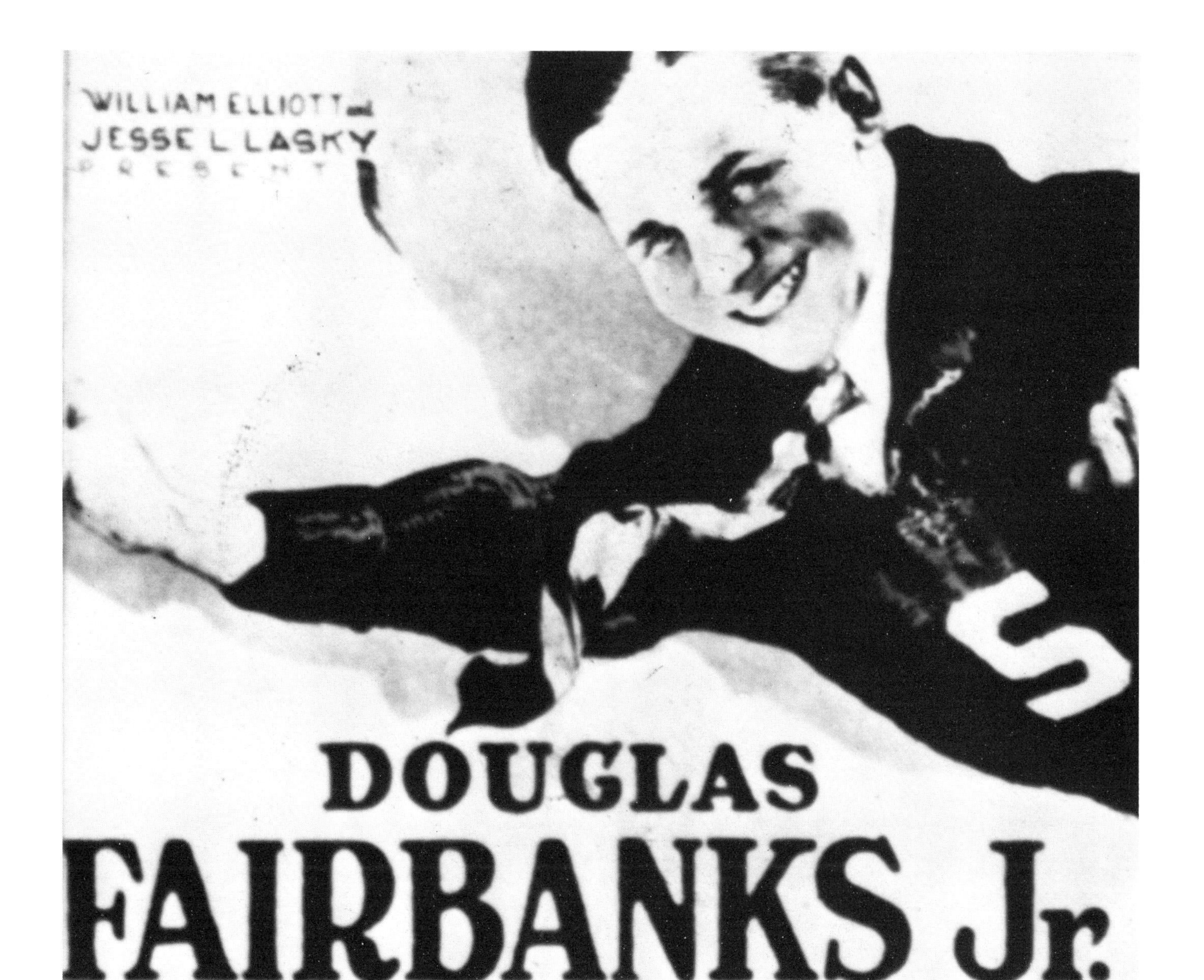
WILLIAM ELLIOTT and
JESSE L LASKY
PRESENT
DOUGLAS
FAIRBANKS Jr.
IN
STEPHEN
STEPS OUT
WITH THEODORE ROBERTS
FROM THE STORY "THE GRAND CROSS OF THE CRESCENT"
WRITTEN FOR THE SCREEN by EDFRID BINGHAM
DIRECTED BY JOSEPH HENABERY
A Paramount Picture

Douglas Fairbanks

"THE THIEF OF BAGDAD"

Even if, in its little way, *Stephen Steps Out* had been worthwhile, it would have seemed small potatoes to Douglas, Sr. He was engaged now in the fascinating business of trying to top himself—with the fantastical *Thief of Bagdad.* Some people were disappointed by the relative lack of acrobatics, and retrospectively its reputation has dimmed, though it is a charming and enchanting work—a movie that always seems to be delighted with itself, as the star seems to be with himself (right).

The Thief of Bagdad, directed by Raoul Walsh (above) in 1923 was Fairbanks' most ambitious production, wildly and wonderfully extravagant, full of special effects that even today have a magical charm about them. The magnificent sets were the work of William Cameron Menzies, who would later do *Gone With the Wind.* Not as overpowering as those for *Robin Hood,* they had an expressionist quality unique in American films at the time, and made a wonderful background for Doug to be at his lightest, most impudent best.

Mechanical Marvels of

By TAMAR LANE

IT is the most perfect piece of movie mechanics that the year has produced, this "Thief of Bagdad," which comes from the studio of Douglas Fairbanks, and in which the incomparable "Doug" takes the leading rôle. The mechanics of it are perfect in spite of the fact that several effects which have never heretofore been attempted by the movie impresarios are used. The success of their workmen and their plans is proved by the fact that even to one accustomed to seeing all the so-called super movies, and educated to all their mechanical tricks, this Bagdad picture holds the illusion. It is as fine a piece of work as a precision observatory clock. Usually, to those accustomed to watch for the mechanics of a production they all turn out to be more or less poorly done mechanically. Not so here.

There were some kinky problems facing the technical director when the plans to film this fantasy were first unveiled in the Fairbanks studio. The cloak of invisibility, the flying carpet, the monster, the flying horse and the magic army were a few of them. This was only a part of the problem, however. There was an idol 300 feet high called for in the script, there were literal acres of castles and cities. Many of these obstacles were simply a matter of mass. Those depicted on these two pages, however, are the ones that demanded ingenuity and a

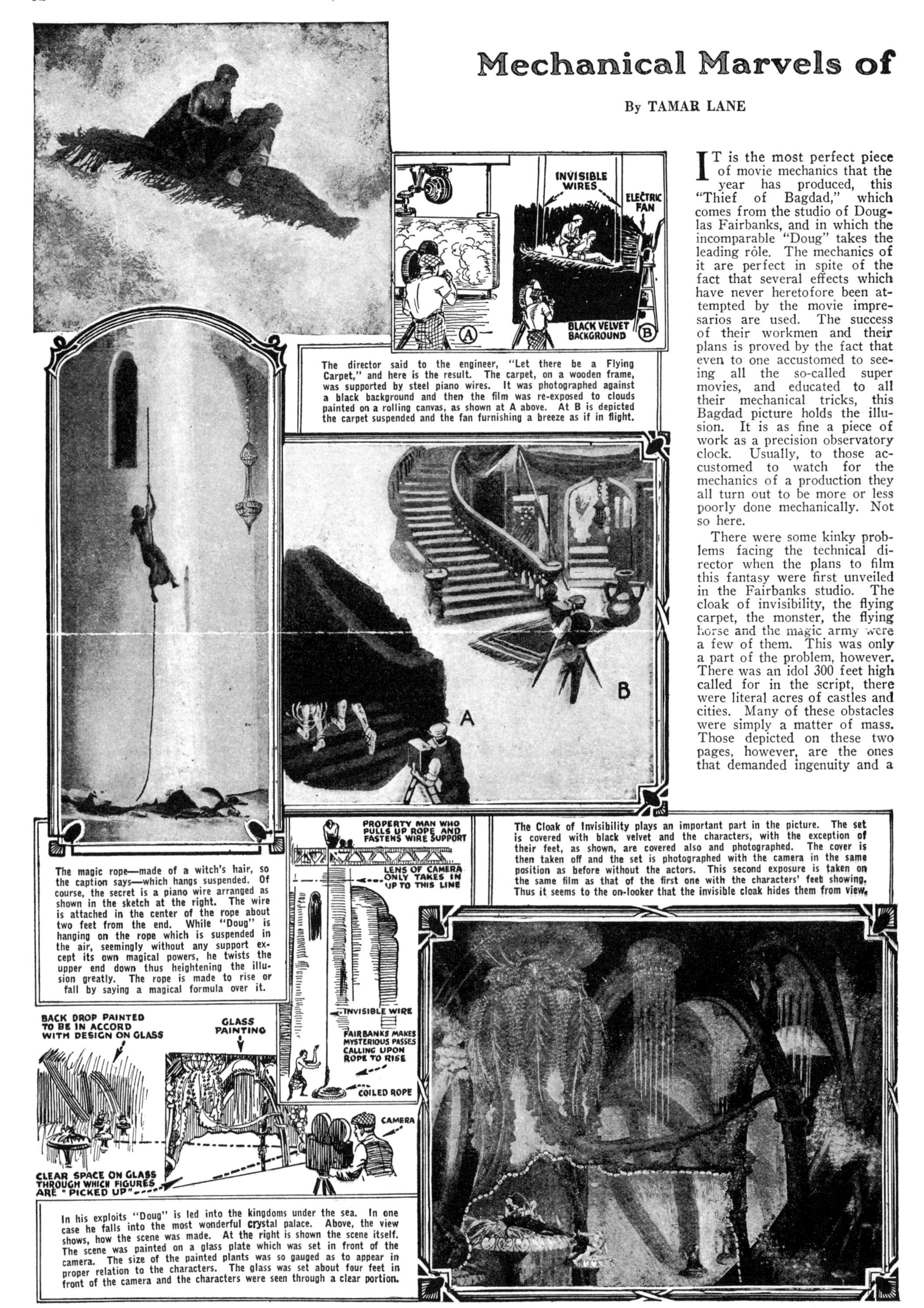

The director said to the engineer, "Let there be a Flying Carpet," and here is the result. The carpet, on a wooden frame, was supported by steel piano wires. It was photographed against a black background and then the film was re-exposed to clouds painted on a rolling canvas, as shown at A above. At B is depicted the carpet suspended and the fan furnishing a breeze as if in flight.

The magic rope—made of a witch's hair, so the caption says—which hangs suspended. Of course, the secret is a piano wire arranged as shown in the sketch at the right. The wire is attached in the center of the rope about two feet from the end. While "Doug" is hanging on the rope which is suspended in the air, seemingly without any support except its own magical powers, he twists the upper end down thus heightening the illusion greatly. The rope is made to rise or fall by saying a magical formula over it.

The Cloak of Invisibility plays an important part in the picture. The set is covered with black velvet and the characters, with the exception of their feet, as shown, are covered also and photographed. The cover is then taken off and the set is photographed with the camera in the same position as before without the actors. This second exposure is taken on the same film as that of the first one with the characters' feet showing. Thus it seems to the on-looker that the invisible cloak hides them from view.

In his exploits "Doug" is led into the kingdoms under the sea. In one case he falls into the most wonderful crystal palace. Above, the view shows, how the scene was made. At the right is shown the scene itself. The scene was painted on a glass plate which was set in front of the camera. The size of the painted plants was so gauged as to appear in proper relation to the characters. The glass was set about four feet in front of the camera and the characters were seen through a clear portion.

"The Thief of Bagdad"

OF HOLLYWOOD, CALIF.

high skill in carrying out the solution once it was devised.

Whether it will be noted by a lay audience or not there is no means of ascertaining, but the fact remains that in every case where a solution to the seemingly miraculous feats was obvious, the director was at pains to show by means of some trick of the actors that the obvious solution was impossible, thereby heightening the illusion. One case of this sort is in connection with the magic rope which hangs suspended in the air with nothing except its magical qualities to hold it.

THE on-looker will immediately think—"Ha, it's easy, there's a wire." Immediately he says it, the illusion is gone and the picture loses its effectiveness. But, the mechanical director obviated his saying it. While "Doug" hangs onto the rope he bends the top of it over, showing that there is no wire attached—or making the audience think that there isn't one—for as a matter of truth there is and a good stout steel one, at that. But little tricks of that type give the picture its perfect finish. Where the mechanics would have been obvious the movie engineers have been careful to hide them. The simplicity of method used in obtaining some extremely gorgeous effects should lead to a lot of credit for the studio staff of designers.

The Flying Horse upon which the Thief rides to the Citadel of the Moon is mystifying, to say the least, until the simplicity with which the scene was made, is explained. The horse and rider were taken against a black background and then the film was rewound and clouds painted on a moving canvas were taken. When developed, a composite view resulted.

SMOKE TUBE

PAPIER MACHE' HORNS STRAPPED ON

There is a terrible monster made by harnessing horns to a crocodile, as shown, and taking an exposure at six feet. "Doug" is then taken on the same film at twenty feet. The distances gives the monstrous size.

STEEL PIANO WIRES

WOODEN PLATFORM COVERED WITH RUG

The flying carpet comes from a window in the Caliph's castle and circles around over the housetops. This is the way it is made to work: The carpet on a wooden frame is suspended by piano wires from a crane. The cameras are placed on the boom and others on adjacent towers. By swinging the carpet and the cameras at the same time an effect of a wide swing is obtained—a much wider sweep than actually is made. The black canopy at the top of the crane is merely a sun shade that was manipulated in order to obtain the proper light effect.

(A) 2. SMOKE POTS IGNITED BY THROWING SWITCH
3. PUFFS PHOTOGRAPHED - 4 FT. OF FILM WOUND BACK

(B) WITH CAMERA STOPPED SOLDIERS TAKE POSITIONS WHERE PUFFS OCCURRED AND CAMERA MAN STARTS PHOTOGRAPHING THEM--GRADUALLY SHARPENING FOCUS

(C) RESULT:- SOLDIERS SEEM GRADUALLY TO MATERIALIZE FROM PUFFS OF SMOKE

A magic chest full of the most wonderful seeds is obtained in the Citadel of the Moon. In fact, with the aid of these seeds one has only to wish and cast a few of them on the ground and behold—In this case it is an army. Each handful of seeds causes a little puff of smoke out of which soldiers materialize. The sketch explains the trick. Electricity sets off the smoke pots. The camera stops and the soldiers step into the smoke. The camera starts again, slightly out of focus. It is brought gradually into sharpness making the soldiers seem to materialize.

It is debatable whether *Thief* was, as Sherwood said on his *Life* page (opposite), "the top" of Fairbanks' art, let alone the movie art. But unquestionably it represented some sort of pinnacle for Fairbanks psychologically. He would not again be quite so lavish, quite so joyously involved in the art and business of movie-making.

"The Thief of Bagdad"

AFTER seeing "The Thief of Bagdad," I am more competent to understand the motives which inspired the sturdy Britons who have been struggling for years to reach the peak of Mt. Everest. I now know what it means to be able to say, "Well, I've been to the top."

Standing at the point marked by this Arabian Nights' entertainment which Douglas Fairbanks has fashioned, I can look down to the lesser summits of "Robin Hood," "Broken Blossoms," "Passion" and the rest; several miles below, and barely discernible from this dizzy altitude, lie "Where Is My Wandering Boy To-night?" "Rags to Riches" and "The Old Nest."

There may well be higher peaks than that achieved by "The Thief of Bagdad"—but if there are, they have not as yet been charted on any of the existent contour maps.

"THE THIEF OF BAGDAD" is the farthest and most sudden advance that the movie has ever made and, at the same time, it is a return to the form of the earliest presentable films. I remember that the first picture I ever saw was a ferociously fast French comedy, in which one of the characters was dressed by magic. His clothes leaped at him from the closet and fitted themselves about his passive form, his boots scurried across the floor and slid onto his feet, and his shoe laces wiggled into place like twin serpents.

That was, technically, "trick stuff"—and it is now sneered at by the hyper-realists of Hollywood, who refuse to admit that a scene is ever faked.

It is trick stuff of this same sort that makes "The Thief of Bagdad" extraordinarily fascinating. Fairbanks has not been afraid to resort to magic of the most flagrant variety. He has used ropes which, when thrown into the air, will become rigid and scalable, golden apples which will restore life to the dead, idols' eyes of crystal in which the future is revealed, magic carpets which fly through the heavens, winged horses, star-shaped keys to open the Palace of the Moon, and golden chests from which vast armies may be conjured with the flick of a finger. There is also a supply of genii, djinns, talismans and fire-breathing dragons.

Of course this wizardry is possible on the screen; the first French comedy proved that. But Fairbanks has gone far beyond the mere bounds of possibility: he has performed the superhuman feat of making his magic seem probable.

When, in "The Ten Commandments," Cecil B. De Mille caused the Red Sea to part, every one remarked, "That's a great trick. How did he do it?" There are no such mental interruptions for the spectator in "The Thief of Bagdad." He watches Fairbanks' phenomenal stunts without stopping to think of them as tricks. He accepts them as facts.

"The Thief of Bagdad" has a marvelous fairy tale quality—a romantic sweep which lifts the audience and vaporizes it into pink, fluffy clouds. It also has much beauty and much solidity of dramatic construction.

Fairbanks and Raoul Walsh, the director, have devised scenes of overwhelming magnitude and grandeur; but, in doing so, they have not neglected the details. They have built, with incredible magnificence, the City of Bagdad—and they have also built a story which is sound and workable, and which proceeds rhythmically and gracefully at a steadily increasing rate of speed.

ONE derives from "The Thief of Bagdad" the same childish thrill that is furnished by a first perusal of Hans Andersen's stories. It is enthrallingly romantic, inspiringly unreal.

If any one can see this marvelous picture and still choose to sneer at the movies, I shall be glad to escort him to Hollywood and feed him to the largest dragon in the Fairbanks menagerie.

Robert E. Sherwood.

If the elder Fairbanks had reached his personal pinnacle in 1924, his son was stuck in a gloomy valley. Laboring under a contract that obliged him to do anything the studio asked, he often found himself acting as a camera assistant—and playing small parts in B pictures. Still, he *was* a Fairbanks, and when he was cast in a film based on Zane Grey's *Wild Horse Mesa,* the famous popular writer was pleased enough to have his picture taken with young Doug (opposite). He, in turn, submitted handsomely to "the build-up" whenever his employers remembered to employ it. Posing for the very collegiate sequence above, he insisted that it include a plug for Betty Bronson, *Photoplay's* cover girl and, briefly, his girl, too. The woman he's embracing is his mother.

Douglas, Jr.'s best break in his early years was as the young man Stella Dallas's daughter marries, while socially unacceptable Mom observes through a glass, rainily, anonymously. But that 1925 loan-out to Samuel Goldwyn did not lead anywhere immediately. Right, looking like the schoolboy he was, he plays Triton in the Miss America sequence of *The American Venus*. Meantime, there was an education to pursue and a family to support, including the once-mighty Daniel Sully, whose uncomplaining acceptance of his humbling fate still moves his grandson. He is seen below sharing a beach umbrella with Beth. Many of Senior's friends were loyal to Junior too—Jack Dempsey, for example.

Douglas Fairbanks, Sr. seemed to his son, as he was growing up, "thoughtless, moody, irritable (at times)," but he cannot remember "a deliberate unkindness." And he was "generous—if he thought of it." One of his first, grand gestures to the boy was the gift of this splendid auto (its make eludes the recipient's memory)—the first young Douglas ever owned. The gift symbolized his father's acceptance of the fact that the young man could not be dissuaded from pursuing a movie career, that Senior was going to try to learn to live with it. Autographed pictures, their inscriptions growing warmer with the passing years (see following pages), demonstrate a further narrowing of the gap between them. In this process, Mary Pickford was a powerful and benign influence on her mercurial, preoccupied husband. (The photo overleaf was her official wedding portrait.)

Famous Players-Lasky Corp.
WEST COAST STUDIO
Paramount Pictures

To Jr.
from Dad
1925

To Junior
from Mary.
1924.

Films like *Man Bait* (above) and *Women Love Diamonds* (opposite), in which Mary Pickford's first husband, Owen Moore, had a featured role, were nothing for Douglas, Jr. to be proud of. But there were consolations. His father had a beach camp at Laguna and he permitted Douglas and friends to use it when he wasn't. This was roughing it, Hollywood-style, and the kids obviously enjoyed it.

While his son toiled in Paramount program pictures, Senior was doing a sequel to his first great historical romance—*Don Q, Son of Zorro.* His co-star was Mary Astor (opposite), his director was Donald Crisp, who stands to the left of his megaphone and his leading man in the photo at right. The star's sword was at the ready throughout, but he perfected a number of memorable stunts involving an Australian stock whip, and they provided the film's most memorable moments.

Comings and goings. They were endless during a period when Hollywood wags insisted that Douglas went to Europe every summer in order to line up Pickfair's guest list for winter. But he was at least as sought after as anyone he sought out. Part of the ritual of their passages, of course, were the attentions of shipboard photographers, one of whom got a rather nice effect above. Below, Maurice Chevalier sees the royal couple off on the Paris boat train in 1925. Opposite, in a Paris garden, circa 1926, they never looked more attractive.

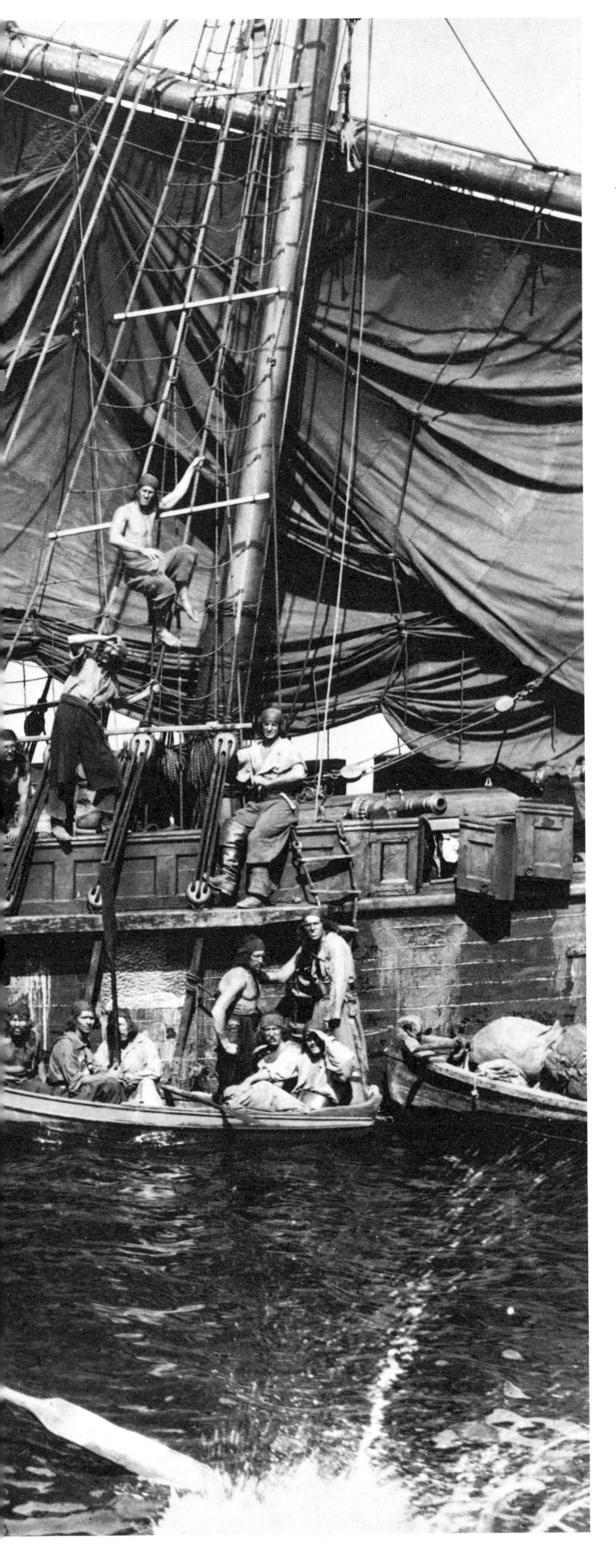

An alert showman, ever ready to experiment with novelties, Fairbanks produced *The Black Pirate* in a new process called Technicolor. It provided him with the gimmick, the unique selling proposition, he was always looking for when he set out to make a spectacular. Freed from the necessity of lingering over special effects (*Bagdad*) or pageantry (*Robin Hood*), he was able to concentrate on lively, straightforward action sequences (overleaf), and many found this return to first principles a refreshment. Whoever had screen credit as writer and director, Doug was first and final arbiter of what went on screen. Stories were always outlined on huge charts on his office wall, his staff aiding the star in adding and subtracting elements over months of pre-production work. No sequence was considered complete until Doug gave the word—generally a laconic "that's it."

The Black Pirate was produced and released simultaneously with Pickford's *Sparrows* and the ad on page 156 didn't lie; this story about a plucky orphan rescuing others like herself from an evil "baby farm" was one of her best. No lie either, one imagines, is the picture with which this chapter concludes. It is one of the few entirely unposed photos of Doug and Mary and suggests the genuine affection and comradeship which lay beneath all the publicity and which would shortly begin to erode.

A Grand New Process - Glorious Technicolor!

Mary Pickford

After all—there is but one Mary Pickford —the brightest name in Motion Picture History.

Now—as though to add emphasis to her leadership, Miss Pickford has produced "Sparrows." The same lovable Mary with her wistful smile, her gay, hoydenish, laughable pranks—but striking a deeper note. This time you see her in a story of tremendous dramatic strength that thrills and stirs with terrific suspense and power.

The Mary Pickford you have always loved is here—but in this picture she is a glowing dramatic figure you have never met. See her as Molly in

UNITED ARTISTS PICTURE
SOON AT YOUR THEATRE
WATCH FOR IT DURING OCTOBER, 1926

Douglas Fairbanks

Pirates! Buried Treasure! Pieces of eight! Fairbanks! The salt tang of the Rovers' sea! The rollicking zest of Doug himself! × ×

Here is a film that will fill your lungs with the adventurous air of Pirate Days. The story of a bold buccaneer's love for a beautiful lady, told against a background of the sweeping sea, armed galleons and the black flag of piracy.

Only Douglas Fairbanks could make such a picture × × ×
In glorious natural colors
[*Technicolor Photography*-]

"THE BLACK PIRATE"

UNITED ARTISTS PICTURE
SOON AT YOUR THEATRE
WATCH FOR IT DURING OCTOBER, 1926

Jayar and Pete

The Gaucho (1927) retained some of the active virtues people expected of a Fairbanks film (below), but as the lovely photo at left suggests it was basically a moody, sombre work, reflecting Fairbanks' deep sense of loss after the death of his eldest brother (and father figure) John, just before production began. Then, too, his own sense—at 44—of mortality beginning to encircle him was perhaps more intense than reasonable. Yet he had staked everything on perpetual youthfulness and now a few critics were cruel enough to point out that he was visibly not a kid anymore. Worse, the year of *The Gaucho's* release was also the year of *The Jazz Singer,* and Fairbanks did not believe his kind of movie-making could withstand the intrusions of dialogue. Or maybe he just did not feel up to facing the creative challenges talk was sure to present him, even though a few years earlier they might have rekindled his essentially enthusiastic nature. Anyway, the film was, if not a flop, a considerable disappointment.

Mary had her own problems with advancing time. The public still saw her and loved her as a perennial *Rebecca of Sunnybrook Farm* (1917, top left) or *Pollyanna* (1920, above), and even in *Sparrows* (1926, left), at 33, she successfully projected that dewey image. But two years later she faced the problem squarely—opposite, she shows off her newly shorn hair to the press. Not coincidentally, she was making *Coquette* at the time—her first grown-up role and a chance to show new range as an actress. The role won her a best-actress award from the young Academy.

380-2

For every fall, a rise: While his father's career wavered, Douglas, Jr. got perhaps the best role of his silent film career, as Garbo's dissolute younger brother in *A Woman of Affairs,* an adaptation of *the* popular novel of the decade, Michael Arlen's *The Green Hat.*

The pictures surrounding *A Woman of Affairs* were also substantially better than their predecessors. Opposite, Doug, Jr. woos Dorothy Mackail in *The Barker*. Above, he appears opposite Loretta Young in his first full sound picture and his first under a new contract with Warner Brothers, which gave him, at last, a steady succession of roles and a coherent publicity build-up establishing him as a performer to be reckoned with in his own right.

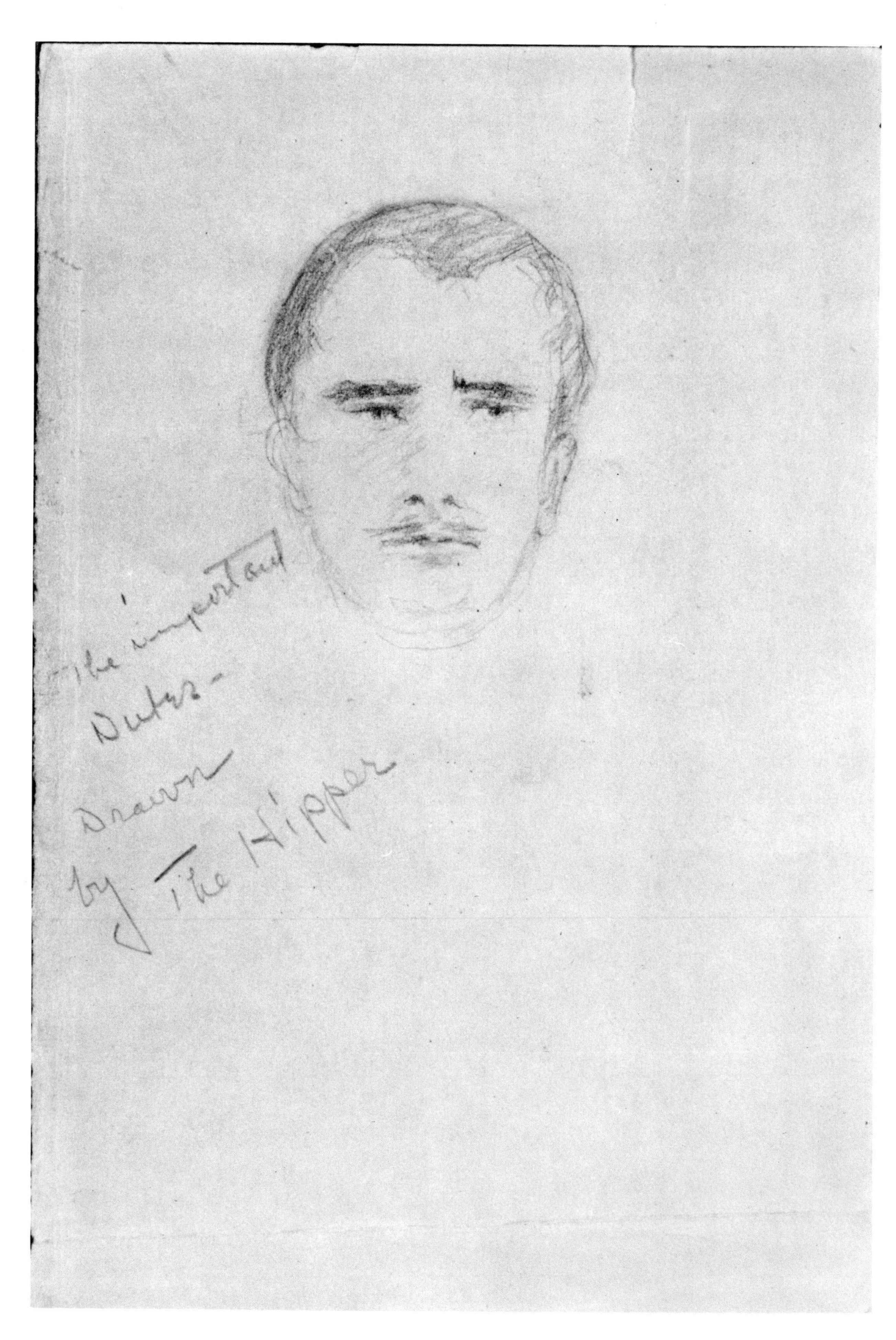

An unexpected talent—Mary Pickford as sketch artist. The date of this drawing is unknown, as are the origins of the pet names by which America's Sweethearts knew each other—"Duber" and "The Hipper."

In the twenties Doug, Jr. wrote sketches of famous friends and relatives for *Vanity Fair*, illustrating them with his caricatures. Clockwise: Garbo, Chaplin, Joan Crawford, John Barrymore, Doug, Sr., and Pickford.

The Iron Mask, made after talkies had been introduced, was Senior's farewell to his beloved D'Artagnan characterization, to the lavish romantic adventure as well. Indeed, it might fairly be said that when he permitted D'Artagnan to die at film's end, he was announcing his own demise as a superstar, though he was only 46. Obviously it was a movie of special importance to him and, just as obviously, he did not stint on production values.

The Iron Mask was directed by Fairbanks' old pal, Allan Dwan, and he has recalled that "Doug seemed to be under some sort of compulsion to make this picture one of his best productions. He had always meticulously supervised every detail of his pictures, but in this one I think he eclipsed himself. It was as if he knew this was his swan song." The film was immoderately expensive (the costume designer alone was paid $40,000; Sir Henry Irving's nephew did the sets) and only moderately successful—though, like Garbo and Chaplin, Fairbanks was one of the few stars who dared fight sound with continued silence and, for the moment at least, he got away with it.

In a city full of beautiful people, no couple was more handsome than Douglas Fairbanks, Jr. and a rising star stage-named Joan Crawford. They met in 1927, quickly became inseparable—despite efforts from all sides of his family to separate them (she was a moody, driving woman, with no social background)—and married in 1929 when Douglas was only 19 and had to lie about his age when they applied for a wedding license. The ceremony took place at St. Malachy's in New York, where they honeymooned for a week (above) before returning to Hollywood. There Nikolas Muray, photographer of the famous in this period (and also Douglas's fencing coach), took the portrait at left—in the process suggesting the golden glow with which memory would come to light this time.

89-605

No less an authority than F. Scott Fitzgerald called Crawford "the best example of the dramatic flapper . . . toying iced glasses with a remote, faintly bitter expression—dancing deliciously—laughing a great deal with wide, hurt eyes." She had made a huge success with *Our Dancing Daughters* in 1928, and seeking to cash in on the publicity deriving from their marriage, M-G-M recruited Doug, Jr. for the sequel, *Our Modern Maidens* (he's driving the car at far left). The marriage lasted only four years, but Fairbanks still regards her as a shaping influence, saving him from being "overwhelmed" by various parental pressures, encouraging him "to strike out on my own in a large way, to grow up and be my own man, independent and challenging."

DF-4

At least one of Junior's parents found himself under a new kind of pressure—the pressure to survive in an industry undergoing radical change just as he was himself suffering what we would now term the mid-life crisis. Mourning for youth now gone, anxious about age closing down his opportunities for new challenges, convinced that talk would interfere with the arc of near-balletic action in the films he liked best to make, a restless, irritable Senior Fairbanks undertook to co-star with his wife in *The Taming of the Shrew* (1929). The leads slightly miscast, their marriage under strain, the film rather static, the picture did nothing to reassure the stars about their future.

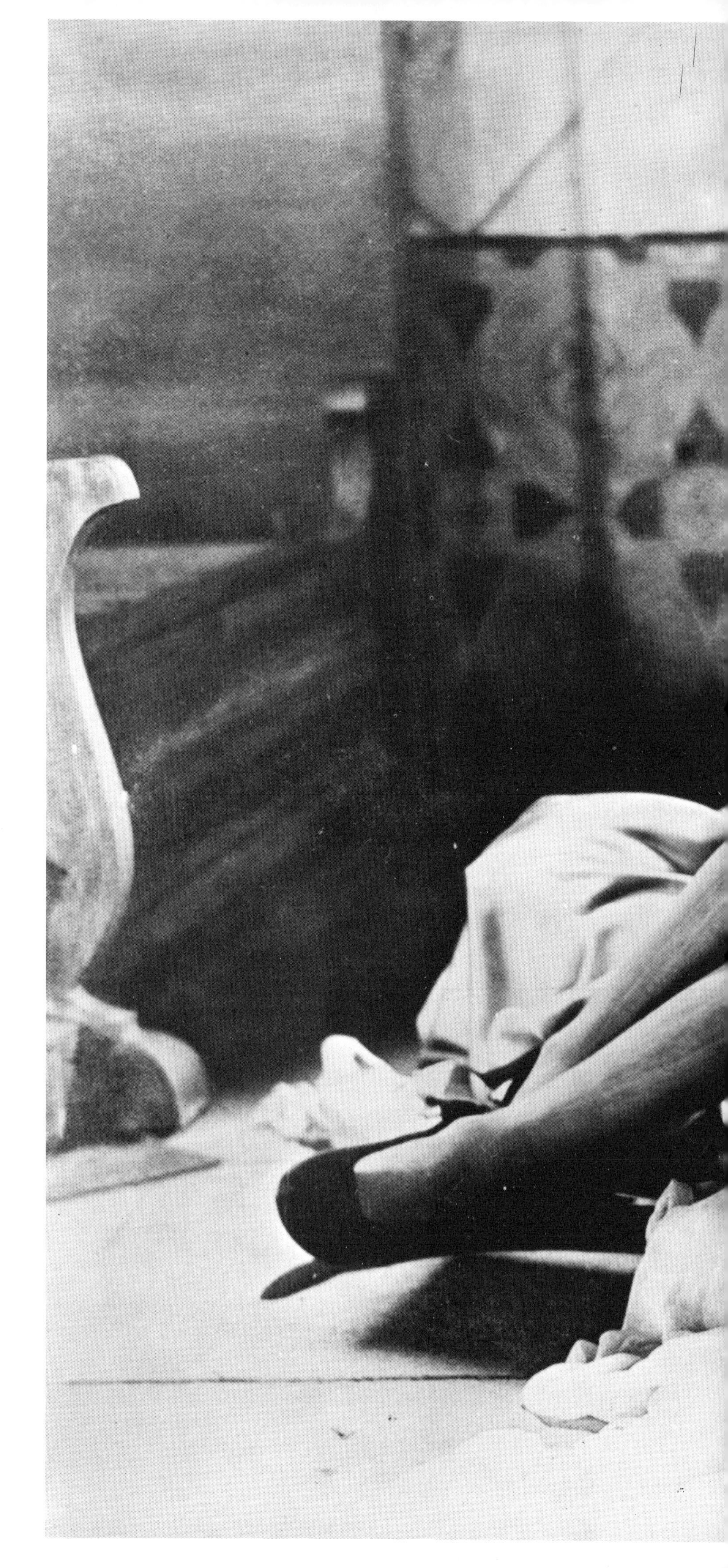

A still that is more than a still. The attitudes they expressed in this scene from *Shrew* were attitudes they expressed in private over the next troubled years: Douglas anguished, Mary trying to be patient and consoling. Their love—or at least the idea that their love was too obviously perfect ever to be totally sundered—survived separation, divorce, perhaps even their remarriages late in the decade.

TS-PF-101. A

At left, Douglas, Mary, and Jack Pickford see Japanese actor Sojin Kamiyama—he was the first feature-film Charlie Chan—off on his homeward voyage. A little later Douglas would follow his wake westward—without Mary. The ostensible purpose was to make a film, *Around the World in Eighty Minutes,* but director Vic Fleming was chosen for the assignment less for his skill than for his amiability, and intimates were shocked that the meticulous Fairbanks would allow such shoddy goods to be placed before the public. But he had a distribution deal to fulfill and no heart for a major creative effort. Below, he could force a smile posing with Duke Kahanamoku, the man who popularized surfing (Jack Pickford at left), but Siamese courtiers, even an elephant ride, failed to lift his mood. When he turned 50 in 1933 Charlie Paddock would write an uplift article on the middle-aged star's ability to achieve joy through strength (overleaf), but its subject would confess to his son the wish for a quick, perhaps violent death.

Douglas Fairbanks

Although Fifty, the Great Star Rides, Boxes, Runs, Swims and Golfs With as Much Enthusiasm and Success as Men Half His Age

THE first time I met Douglas Fairbanks he challenged me to a race. That was more than ten years ago when I thought that I could run pretty well. After the match I was not so sure. Douglas made it a real battle, beating me at the start and fighting gamely every foot of the way.

Later, I was to find that Fairbanks was a better boxer than he was a runner and a greater gymnast than he was a boxer. Today, on the borderline of fifty, he is the most astonishing all-around athlete for his age that I have ever known or heard about. Yet he is not dependent upon unusual speed or weight. If he lived the kind of life that most successful business men indulge in, he would probably be slow and balance the scales around one hundred and ninety pounds. Fairbanks has big bones, large shoulders, a splendid pair of legs and tremendous muscles—and weighs less than one hundred and fifty pounds!

Douglas and I have been friends in sport for a long time, but of late we have not had the opportunity of playing very much together, and I thought possibly that in approaching what most men consider as middle age, Douglas might have lost his enthusiasm for strenuous physical exercise. So, not long ago, I spent a day with him and discovered to my surprise that his schedule was as arduous as ever.

We were called at six-thirty in the morning, and before seven we were mounted and galloping toward the mountains behind Beverly. We rode hard for half an hour, drinking deep of the crisp morning air. Upon our return we changed into bathing shorts, took a turn in a pool of water which was magnificently cold, and were ready for breakfast at eight. We did not eat a great deal. A cup of coffee, some fruit and dry toast, sufficed Fairbanks. By nine o'clock we were at the studio, and from then until late in the afternoon Douglas devoted himself to business.

At four o'clock he was ready to play, and from then until seven, as is his daily custom, he thoroughly enjoyed himself. These three hours are the ones Fairbanks lives for. The thrill of picture success, the art of creating a story, the glamour of action, the applause of the world lack that something which these three hours supply. From four until seven, every day but

Charles Paddock, crack runner and hurdler, is compelled to "step along" when Doug Fairbanks and Charlie Chaplin hit the cinder trail

In "Reaching for the Moon," as everywhere else, Mr. Fairbanks takes his place high above all others in the fields of acting and athletics

RECREATION

at 50

By
Charles W. Paddock
The Famous Olympic Sprints Champion

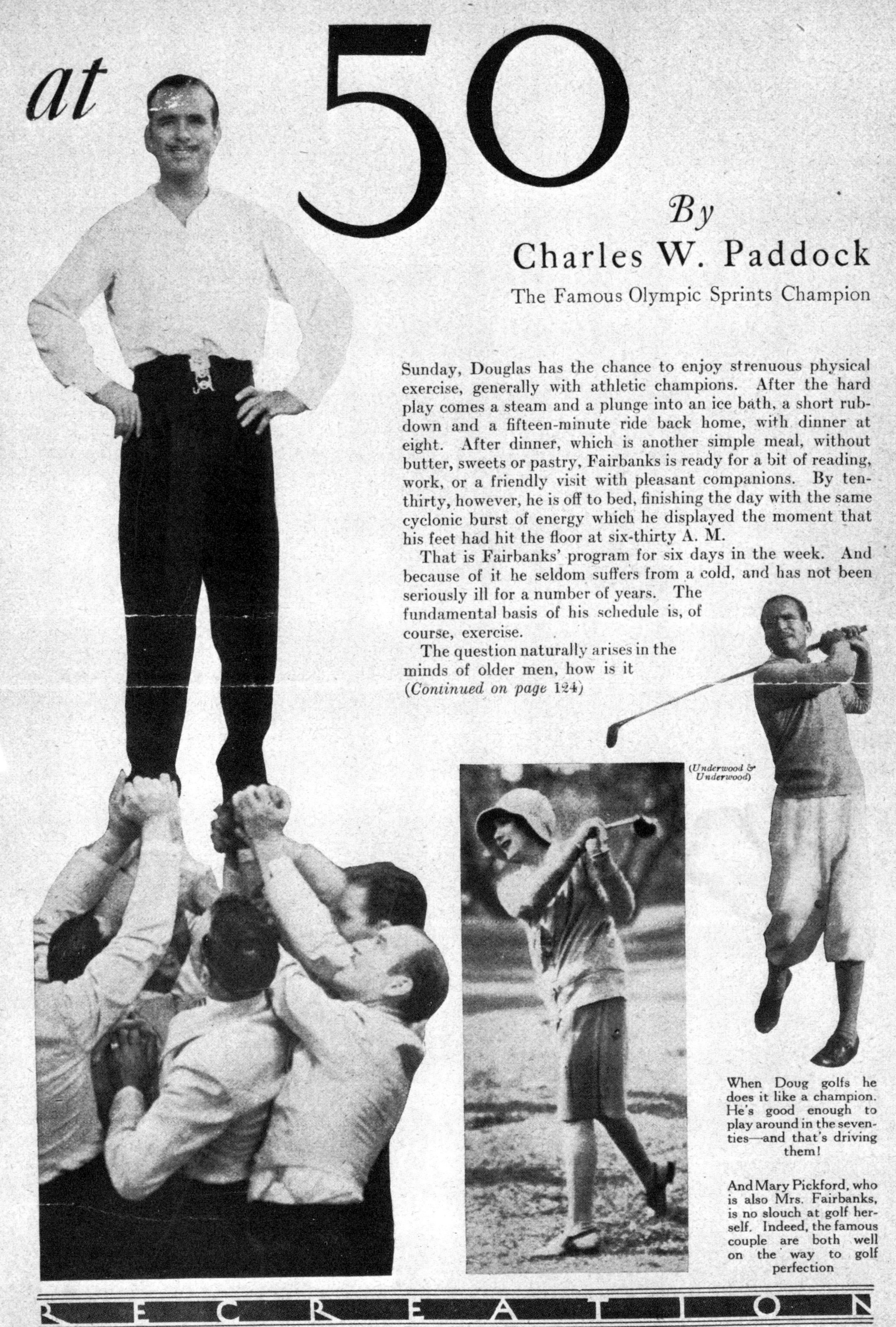

Sunday, Douglas has the chance to enjoy strenuous physical exercise, generally with athletic champions. After the hard play comes a steam and a plunge into an ice bath, a short rub-down and a fifteen-minute ride back home, with dinner at eight. After dinner, which is another simple meal, without butter, sweets or pastry, Fairbanks is ready for a bit of reading, work, or a friendly visit with pleasant companions. By ten-thirty, however, he is off to bed, finishing the day with the same cyclonic burst of energy which he displayed the moment that his feet had hit the floor at six-thirty A. M.

That is Fairbanks' program for six days in the week. And because of it he seldom suffers from a cold, and has not been seriously ill for a number of years. The fundamental basis of his schedule is, of course, exercise.

The question naturally arises in the minds of older men, how is it
(*Continued on page 124*)

(*Underwood & Underwood*)

When Doug golfs he does it like a champion. He's good enough to play around in the seventies—and that's driving them!

And Mary Pickford, who is also Mrs. Fairbanks, is no slouch at golf herself. Indeed, the famous couple are both well on the way to golf perfection

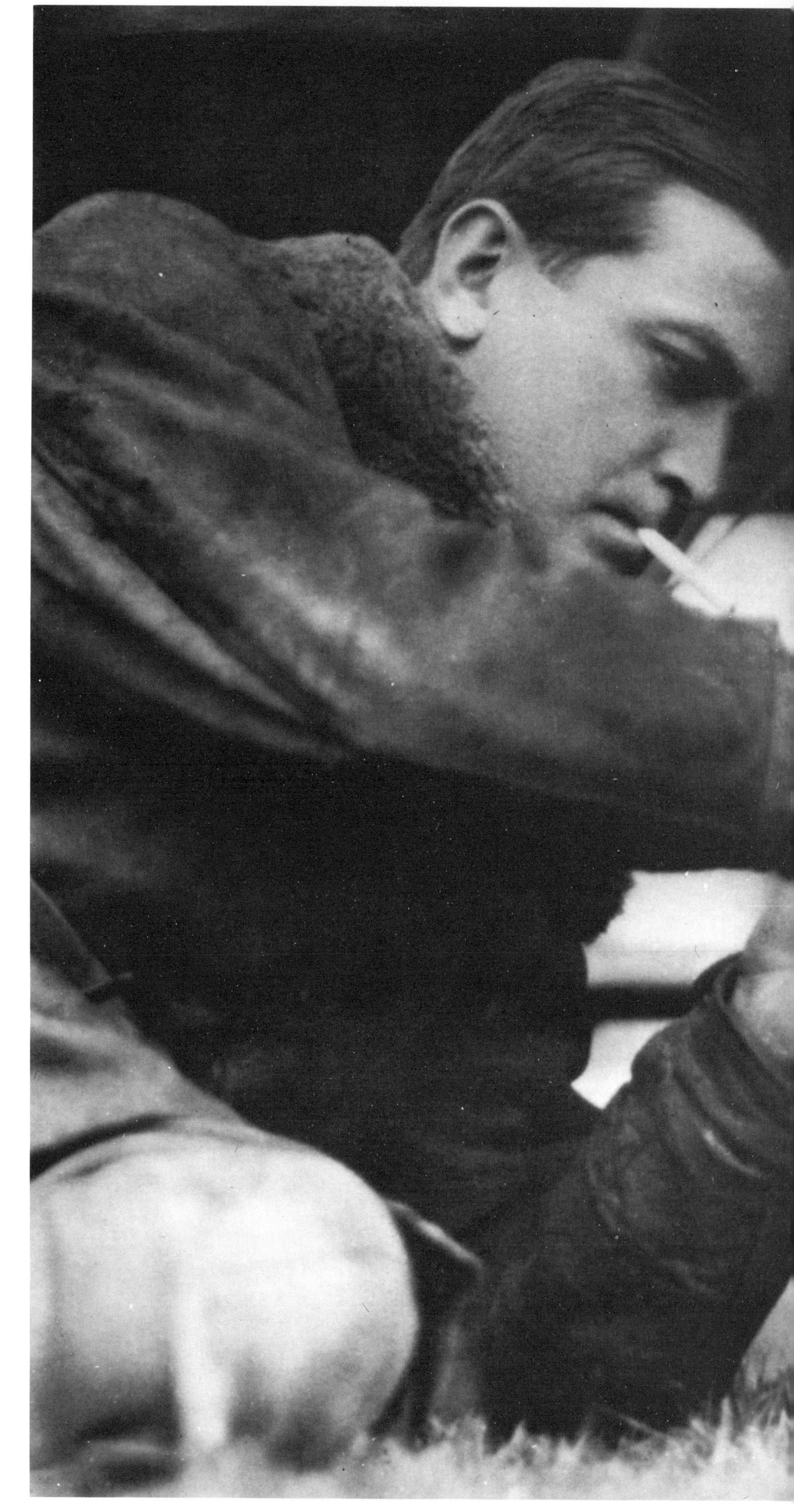

While his father floundered, the well-spoken younger Fairbanks flourished before the sound cameras. He made a particularly strong impression with Richard Barthelmess in *The Dawn Patrol* under Howard Hawks' direction in 1930, winning a long-term Warner contract as a result.

"Jayar" (as his father took to calling him around this time) scored strongly again in 1931, as the gigolo in *Little Caesar,* taking it from Eddie G. (left), dishing it out to Glenda Farrell (above). The studio rewrote his contract, permitting him to work less, have more control over what he did. The orgy in 1932's *Scarlet Dawn* (opposite) looks more interesting than it was, while 1933's *Parachute Jumper* (below) was the sort of routine programmer that drove his outspoken co-star, Bette Davis, crazy. Less afflicted by temperament, and having worked in far worse to support his family, Jayar took such jobs equably.

A study in contrasts. In 1933 Douglas, Jr. and Mickey Rooney shared a film, *The Life of Jimmy Dolan,* and a backlot heater warding off the morning chill. It was a "realistic" picture, typical of Warner Brothers' routine style at the time. And Fairbanks was now growing restive with the material he was getting and a salary cut he and other stars had been asked to take but which the studio was slow to restore when better times returned. A loan-out to RKO, where he appeared opposite Katherine Hepburn in *Morning Glory,* represented a welcome change of pace, but she got most of the glory—and her first Oscar. Relations between Fairbanks and the studio started to slide rapidly downhill from that point onward and within the year they would agree to a separation. Coincidentally, this was also the year in which his marriage to Crawford ended.

Jayar might have his ups and downs at the studio, but on film there was nothing but downs for "Pete," as his father liked his son to call him. *Mr. Robinson Crusoe* (1932) was another attempt to combine business with pleasure, this time by hiring a splendid yacht, cruising to Tahiti and making an updated version of the Defoe novel. The result has been described as "disastrously unworthy" of the elder Fairbanks, though family tradition has it that Jayar soon thereafter had several unacknowledged half-brothers on the island. Be that as it may, father and son, their careers simultaneously at an ebb, would soon make common cause—happily so for Jayar, whose career would revive and who would at last find rapport with a father who had too long been too distant.

Of troubles at Pickfair in the early thirties the public knew nothing, as publicity shots rolled onward unstinted. Above, Al Jolson, Doug, Mary, Ronald Colman, Sam Goldwyn celebrate opening of a line between Hollywood and British production centers while Eddie Cantor—literally—holds the phone. Below, Doug, dice, a lucky M. Chevalier.

Even the more intimate shots revealed nothing. Above the two Dougs escort Mary to a football game and, a little later, enjoy a ski weekend at Lake Arrowhead. People didn't seem to notice that Doug, Sr. was rarely in one place for any length of time or that Mary was only rarely seen beside him.

One of Fairbanks' last Warner releases was *Captured* (left), a POW drama in which he co-starred with Leslie Howard and Paul Lukas. More important to him was his friendship with John Barrymore, seen below in his Rasputin get-up, meeting a Pickfair guest, the Duke of Sutherland. The great actor "treated me as if I were a contemporary," and when youthful crises occurred "gave me better, friendlier advice than I could get from my usually self-conscious father."

"Dickie" Mountbatten, later to become Britain's great naval commander in World War II, was an early Fairbanks intimate (below). He blended cool courage with great kindness. Boyish, romantic, a lover of games, gadgets and grand strategies, his unabashed drive, need to prove himself, encouraged Doug to be at least a little more open about his own similar need to achieve on his own. As for "Larry," Fairbanks quickly perceived the greatness of his gift.

"All the News That's Fit to Print."

VOL. LXXXII....No. 27,554.

Entered as Second-Class Matter, Postoffice, New York, N. Y.

Jayar and Pete (even now the senior Fairbanks did not like calling a son a son, or being addressed as a father), sailed for England in 1933 to make films they hoped would impart new directions to their careers. While they were abroad, rumors of a split between Doug and Mary were finally publicly confirmed—and even the then stuffy *Times* played the story high. Among other things, Mary was suffering one of the most horrid cases of golf widowhood on record, as the lower clipping and pictures opposite indicate. But more than a game had come between them, of course. He was a badly shaken man, his career in disarray, his fortune diminished by the Depression, and he possessed neither the will nor the ideas to set things right.

It is impossible, in brief space, to trace Doug and Mary's international efforts to patch things up, but over the next few years they frequently flew dramatically to each other's side, were thwarted by everything from timetables to mislaid telegrams in their attempts to renew a marriage in which the whole world had a romantic stake. These were sad, silly years for Douglas, Sr., and it may be that the only good thing about them was his growing closeness with, even dependency on, his son. In the end, one cannot help but think he was determined to destroy himself, that there was nothing Mary, Doug, Jr., their many anxiously hovering friends, could do to help him. They could not give him—any more than he could himself—what he wanted and missed, the youthfulness on which, for him, everything had always depended and which now, at last, had deserted and betrayed him.

New York Times.

LATE CITY EDITION

WEATHER—Probably rain today; tomorrow fair, slightly warmer. Temperatures yesterday—Max., 71; min., 65.

Copyright, 1933, by The New York Times Company.

NEW YORK, MONDAY, JULY 3, 1933. P TWO CENTS In New York City. | THREE CENTS Within 200 Miles | FOUR CENTS Elsewhere Except in 7th and 8th Postal Zones

Mary Pickford Reveals Break With Husband Douglas Fairbanks

Pickfair, $500,000 Home at Beverly Hills, Is Put Up for Sale—Fairbanks in London Is Reported Spending the Week-End With Prince of Wales.

Special to THE NEW YORK TIMES.

LOS ANGELES, July 2.—The "house of happiness" of Douglas Fairbanks and Mary Pickford has fallen and separation of the two famous motion picture stars is contemplated. Tearfully Miss Pickford confirmed today rumors of the separation, with the announcement that Pickfair Beverley Hills mansion that has been a show place of the film world for many years, is for sale.

Miss Pickford summed up the whole story of the rift between her and her husband in the following brief statement issued through her personal representative, after efforts to see her had failed:

"It is true that Pickfair is for sale and that a separation between Douglas and me is contemplated. If there should be a divorce the grounds will be incompatibility. Beyond that there is nothing further to say."

A statement was attributed to her personal representative that no attorney has been engaged to handle the "contemplated" separation and that "no action is being taken at the present time."

It was pointed out that the sale of Pickfair has been under consideration on several previous occasions.

The statement did not indicate whether the previously contemplated sale of Pickfair was due to marital difficulties.

Mr. Fairbanks is in London on one of his European trips. His traveling in recent years without

Continued on Page Five.

The Fairbankses, an inappropriately garbed companion, and heavyweight champ Max Schmeling head linksward.

Wales and Doug Lose

Finish Behind Prince George and Archie Compston on English Links.

SUNNINGDALE, Eng., June 19 (AP).—The Prince of Wales and Douglas Fairbanks today paired in a golf foursome but came out second best to Prince George and Archie Compston, British professional.

Compston and Wales' younger brother defeated the monarch-to-be and the American movie actor 3 and 2.

The match was close all the way but Fairbanks and the Prince lost three straight holes, after making the turn all square, and could not regain the lost ground.

Herald Tribune photos—Acme

They were both working with Alexander Korda, Hungarian hope of the backward British film industry. He, like the Fairbankses, enjoyed historical spectacles and he put Douglas in *Catherine the Great,* where he was excellent as a mad monarch (below). H. G. Wells, fascinated as ever by the wonders of modernism, was a frequent visitor to the set, gathering firsthand information about the miracle of the movies (right).

Senior's picture was *The Private Life of Don Juan,* in which he portrayed an aging Don, disappointingly unable to live up to his youthful reputation. Some critics liked the picture, but the public didn't—and it was his last. His co-star was Merle Oberon (Mrs. Korda), and he joined her and her husband for a seemingly carefree Swiss holiday—though he lacked proper sledding costume.

THE SORROWS OF DIERDRE IN "THE WINDING JOURNEY"

MR. DOUGLAS FAIRBANKS, Jr. (MICHAEL) AND MISS GERTRUDE LAWRENCE (DIERDRE)

Philip Leader's ultra-modern problem play, with a most uncomfortable ending for the husband (Michael) and a problematical future for the wife (Dierdre), was presented at the Opera House, Manchester, on May 7, and is due in London in about three weeks' time. It is scarcely a cheerful story, but is what is called a good acting play for both the people principally concerned—Gertrude Lawrence, the modern wife with a previous attachment who goes on paying her bills as before, and Douglas Fairbanks, the young man also with an attachment in the shape of a lady who is about to have a baby. Michael discovers about the bills, and, coming on top of the other affair, they are too much for him, and he shoots himself, leaving Dierdre free to go on having her bills paid by the accommodating other gentleman

Photographs by Dorothy Wilding

During this first, extended professional stay in London, Douglas, Jr. twice played opposite Gertrude Lawrence on stage—in *The Winding Journey* and (below) *Moonlight is Silver* by Clemence Dane. Their plays did not prosper greatly—and neither did a movie they made together, *Mimi*—but their off-stage relationship did. The names of Gertrude Lawrence and Douglas Fairbanks, Jr. were linked for two years. In London they cruised the Thames in his motor launch; on one of their continental tours a matador dedicated a bull to the couple. It was all rather gay, even Noel Coward-ish.

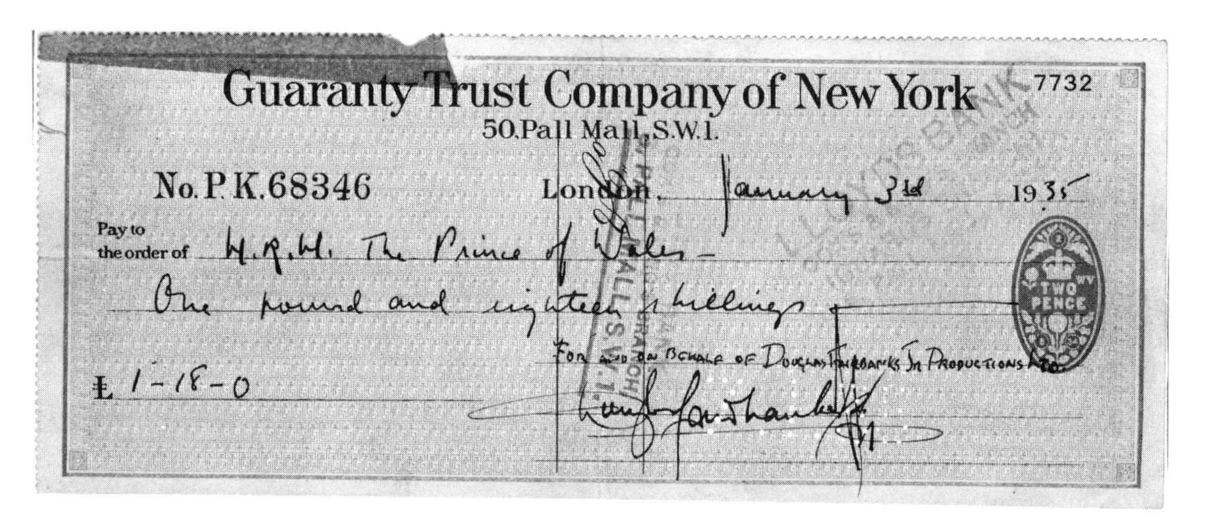
Guaranty Trust Company of New York 7732
50 Pall Mall, S.W.1.

No. P.K.68346 London, January 3rd 1935

Pay to the order of H.R.H. The Prince of Wales —

One pound and eighteen shillings

For and on behalf of Douglas Fairbanks Jr Productions Ltd.

£ 1-18-0

TWO PENCE

For Douglas, Jr. this was a very good time. The films he made in London didn't amount to much, but the friendships he made there did. He proudly kept a check recording a minor loss to a major figure in a poker game (top), counted Noel Coward and Clemence Dane (left) as major influences on his life. Her portrait of him was done in the sixties, but the qualities he admired in her were evidenced early on. She was a "woman of wisdom, wild enthusiasm . . . a beautiful soul of great and varied talent"—this eccentric novelist, poet and painter.

11 WELLINGTON SQUARE CHELSEA S W 3 SLO 4439

Epitaph
on
Douglas Fairbanks, Junior.

When I am dead, say only that I lived
Each moment fully, squeezed each minute dry
Into Time's cup, and drank it! Say that I,
Whatever grief pursued me, never grieved
But in the darkest hour of night believed
In the white dawn, that soon should flood the sky.
Defeated, kept my faith in Victory,
And all my loss by one bold stroke retrieved.

Say that I died, died fighting, fighting yet,
Though beaten backward, bleeding, to the ground;
That no remorse, repentance or regret
Darkened my parting spirit — for I found
In that sharp pang that comes to every one
No pain at all, except that Life was done.

James Laver
14. 11. 35

James Laver, who died as this book was being prepared, would gain fame as one of the world's most sensible and engaging historians of fashion and manners. As a younger man he composed this epitaph to a young man whose high spirits and infinite worldly curiosity seemed to flourish more openly in England than they ever had on his native shores.

In England, Douglas, Jr. discovered that he could be his own producer. His first—and quite good—film was *The Amateur Gentleman.* His father, shown below visiting the set, was very encouraging about this show of independence. Right, the co-star of his second production, *Accused,* was Dolores Del Rio, and when it was over he saw her off on the new *Queen Mary's* second voyage. His mother and her husband, Jack Whiting, were coincidental fellow passengers.

A fit-looking Fairbanks, Sr. escorts Darryl Zanuck—whose finery is as obviously rented as Douglas's is bespoke—to Ascot (left). By this time he had met a former show girl who had become Lady Ashley. The portrait below gives some idea of the cool elegance that attracted Fairbanks (and, later, Clark Gable, to whom she was briefly wed).

The charade ends. Even after his final divorce decree was granted, Mary telegraphed a reconciliation offer to Doug in New York—but a hotel room clerk misfiled it and Doug had proposed to the (now) former Lady Ashley and taken ship to join her before his son could get the message to him. His dress remained dapper, his stride firm, but one could not see in him any longer the jaunty, mischievous young man a nation had taken to its heart. Nor was the middle-aged woman emerging from divorce court recognizably America's Sweetheart. They were indistinguishable now from any other prosperity-ravaged pair.

Making it official. Having been seen in many of the continent's best watering places (opposite, at an Ostia restaurant, just arrived from St. Moritz), Fairbanks, Sr. and Sylvia, whose former husband had been very unpleasant about granting a divorce, were finally married in France. Ambassador Jesse Straus and Elizabeth Govat were the witnesses. A little later, Mary Pickford and Buddy Rogers were receiving as newlyweds at Pickfair (below). She is shaking hands with Gwynne Rupp, her sister Lottie's child, whom Mary adopted.

What can one say? The photographers were now less numerous at his comings and goings, but the sudden glare of their flashbulbs was often unspeakably cruel—and profoundly revealing. One recoils from the emotional void.

Of course, front was kept up—particularly on formal occasions. Above, Fairbanks and bride join Norma Shearer and Irving Thalberg, successors to the title of Hollywood's reigning couple, on an outing. The clippings are typical of the period, Fairbanks determinedly pretending to activity as a producer, though his heart was not in it and all of his projects finally came to nothing.

Fairbanks, the Producer

By Marguerite Tazelaar

DOUGLAS FAIRBANKS, who last appeared on the screen five years ago in "Don Juan," will start work on a new picture, "The Adventures of Marco Polo," this spring. But it will not be as an actor; it will be as co-producer with Samuel Goldwyn.

"I have never been an actor, really," he said. "I've just been kidding the public all these years. I'm a business man; always have been. Producing is my line. I've produced my own pictures, planned the stories and directed from my office. Of course, I surround myself with the best people I can get."

To say that Mr. Fairbanks looked "in the pink" would be superfluous, for he always looks that way. As slight of figure as he was in "Robin Hood," "The Thief of Bagdad" or "The Taming of the Shrew," the brown-faced man who "follows the sun" has aged less than most of his contemporaries. His erect figure was draped in a black lounging suit, and he was wearing a black Russian blouse buttoned tight around the neck, and black velvet slippers with his initials in white embroidered on the toes.

The Mobile Fairbanks

He appears unable to remain stationary more than two minutes at a time, and as he talks he walks rapidly. He remarked for no apparent reason that there was an old Chinese motto which said, "Never stand up when you can sit down, and never sit down when you can lie down," whereupon he continued to pace.

He set forth a theory about relaxing which he said a Yogi had taught him. It was a little difficult to follow, but it seems that by projecting your mental processes into space, as it were, for a few minutes, whether you are conversing or resting on a divan, you will be able, providing you can completely empty your mind, to get the refreshment of many hours of sleep. Mr. Fairbanks may have been practicing on his visitor, because he certainly seemed brimming with relaxation, ideas and vitality.

China Is a Natural

He has been planning to make "The Adventures of Marco Polo" for some time, his travels in China having been extensive.

"I've been all over the Polo ground, as it were," he said, "and the period appealed to me. It's set about 700 years ago. I'm sending a unit to China for process shots. We'll start the picture in Hollywood about May 1, and hope to release it in the fall. No color! To make it in black and white will be a hard enough job."

Mr. Fairbanks hoped to have his son play the lead, but the latter was booked up, so Gary Cooper was signed. Basil Rathbone will have an important role, and Sigrid Gurie, Norwegian screen star, probably will play the feminine lead. Mr. Fairbanks is producing it with Goldwyn because "Goldwyn has the producing organization which I lack."

He's for Hollywood

He said he thought Hollywood was the best place to produce pictures. In London and New York there are so many distractions that work cannot be carried on with such concentration as it can in the city where the making of films is the sole occupation and diversion, he said.

"In Hollywood an actor, director or executive never stops working during his waking hours," Mr. Fairbanks said. "At dinner he talks shop, and nearly every party breaks up in a picture conference. I figure each individual works five hours longer in Hollywood for the screen, every day, than he does in London or would in New York."

As for the future of pictures:

"I'm the world's worst prophet. I said when talking pictures first started that they would not go unless eighty per cent was motion and twenty per cent dialogue. And yet, behold! Personally, I always try to shave down talk, and expect to in this new production. It seems to me a picture should always keep moving. As to color, it's all right if it can be worked out, if it will intensify the drama. But the results so far have been far from perfect. The reactions we get from nature's coloring are not the same as those we get from the screen. We must breed an artist who will give us the same emotional reaction, and this may take time. At present, I think Walt Disney is the greatest color artist there is."

FAIRBANKS SAYS CAREER IS OVER

Ex-Star Admits He's Too Old for Hollywood—Sails Aboard Normandie.

Douglas Fairbanks, Sr., confessed somewhat sadly today that he'll never appear in a motion picture again because he's too old.

Mr. Fairbanks, once one of the brightest stars of Hollywood, sailed aboard the French liner Normandie with Mrs. Fairbanks, the former Lady Ashley.

"So far as I am personally concerned," the former jumping jack of Hollywood said, "I'm through with pictures. I'm too old. The movies have left me behind. In my days on the silent screen things were entirely different than they are today. I'll leave it to my son and younger men and women to carry on."

Mr. Fairbanks took a print of the new film, "The Prisoner of Zenda," aboard the ship and said he will preside at the first premiere of a motion picture ever held at sea. Douglas Fairbanks, Jr., has a leading role in the film.

A party of twelve, the entire population of Zenda, Ont., led by Mayor Vernon Fewster, arrived at Floyd Bennett Field today in a single transport plane to see the New York premiere of the "Prisoner of Zenda" at Radio City Music Hall. Zenda was named for the Anthony Hope novel.

Douglas, Jr.'s producing venture failed after a couple of flops, but he took his father's advice ("Rin-Tin-Tin couldn't miss in that part") and signed on to play the wicked Rupert of Hentzau in Selznick's fine production of *The Prisoner of Zenda.* The idea of never appearing in anything but black was his own, and he stole the show from heroic Ronald Colman. Right, they talk things over with co-director John Cromwell.

A silly season: Between the romance of *Zenda* and the derring-do of his next, perhaps most memorable, film, Douglas, Jr. joined Irene Dunne in 1938 in a likable light comedy, *The Joy of Living* (left and top), co-starred with Ginger Rogers above a supporting cast that included Jack Carson and Lucille Ball in *Having Wonderful Time,* strolled between takes of *The Young in Heart* with Paulette Goddard and fine-feathered friend.

S.I.P-106-P-198

Gunga Din (1939) was one film that lived up to the industry slogan that Fairbanks and other heavies help promote above. Directed by George Stevens, it also starred Cary Grant, Victor McLaglen, Joan Fontaine, with Sam Jaffe in the title role (at left, below)—only a featured player's role in this free adaptation of Kipling's poem.

Douglas Fairbanks, Jr. met his second wife briefly when she visited Hollywood in 1938 and was still married to Huntington Hartford. They met again on New Year's Day, 1939, at a country house party given by Herbert Bayard Swope, just an hour after Hartford and the former Mary Lee Epling of Virginia had agreed to a divorce during a phone conversation. They married in Los Angeles just months later, with "Pete" in attendance as best man, celebrity friends sending best wishes in a variety of amusing forms, and Lolly Parsons setting her stamp of approval on the whole business by writing what passed for a think piece about what marriages did to careers and vice versa in Hollywood. Cast and crew of the picture he was working on at the time, *Rulers of the Sea,* conspired to half-convince the groom that as the production was behind schedule he might not be excused from the set in time to meet his bride at the altar. In short, they may have been an atypical movie-capital couple, but their wedding was typical of time and place.

No 'Career' Problem for Doug, Jr. This Tim

Young Fairbanks' Marriage Today to Southern Socialite Raises Discussion of Actor-Actress Romance Peril

By LOUELLA O. PARSONS,
Motion Picture Editor International News Service.
Copyright, 1939, by International News Service.

HOLLYWOOD, April 22.

YOUNG Douglas Fairbanks, who has had more romances with actresses than almost any other Hollywood hero, is casting no reflections on the former "career women" in his life by marrying a non-professional.

"I'm not marrying an actress because I happ:ned to fall in love with a girl who isn't one," Doug gallantly told us yesterday over the phone, just 24 hours before he and Mrs. Mary Hartford step down the aisle at the Methodist Church in Beverly Hills.

But I remember at the time Doug and Joan Crawford were separated he said that he doubted if he would ever again try marriage with an actress. That was no reflection on Joan—it was just that he felt two careers under one roof was too much of a strain on any marriage.

Well, this afternoon Doug, Jr., will follow out that belief when he takes the Southern socialite as his bride. Her only interest in a movie studio is visiting her husband on the set now and then—and that not too often, even though they will start their honeymoon on "location" at Catalina.

Doug's marriage to a non-professional again brings up the interesting problem of "career" brides vs. the non-professional variety. Lately there has been a run of actor-actress marriages—Florence Rice and Robert Wilcox, Carole Lombard and Clark Gable, while Bob Taylor and Barbara Stanwyck are expected to take the big step any day now.

Tarzan to Wed Non-Professional

Johnny Weissmuller, however, after five hectic years of matrimony with Lupe Velez, is another screen hero who, like Douglas, will take a non-professional bride for his second venture when he marries Beryl Scott some time this Summer.

Other noted advocates of "one career under one roof" are the Fred MacMurrays, the Bing Crosbys, the Fred Astaires, Pat O'Briens, James Cagneys, Gary Coopers.

Only the immediate family and close friends will attend the Fairbanks ceremony this afternoon and I'm sure my feminine readers are interested in an advance peek at what the bride will wear. She will look like a breath of Spring in a rose-beige silk jersey ensemble created by Alix, with a full circular skirt. Her Chanel hat of blue is trimmed with pink and white phlox with a long white dotted veil giving the necessary bride-like effect. Royal blue suede pumps, white kid gloves and a white bag complete the ensemble—except for the bridal bouquet of Sprir.g flowers.

"A woman of strong character, but with an infinite capacity for love and loyalty for close friends and family. The only world for her is the one in which they live. She has a highly developed sense of humor, good taste and is easily adaptable to circumstances, a stubborn insistence on what is right and wrong." Thus Douglas Fairbanks, Jr. on his wife, 35 years after these pictures were taken while he worked (opposite) with Margaret Lockwood on *Rulers of the Sea.* Doting sentiment? To an objective observer they seem an acutely accurate description of a strong, intelligent, and entirely remarkable woman.

The other marriage: He could still vault a paddock fence, hit a Palm Spring pool with an oddly graceless eagerness. But friends noted a lost quality about him when they met him unexpectedly. And when the chill came on him at an outdoor party and he draped his wife's fur about him, the candid photographer caught Douglas Fairbanks, Sr. as he had never been seen before—looking smaller than life. One weekend he attended a football game, came to a party at his son's house, then was stricken by what seemed a mild heart attack. He rallied briefly, but as his son and a few others had known for years, he did not really care anymore about living. In the first hour of Dec. 12, 1939, he managed some false cheer for an inquiring nurse: "I've never felt better." By morning, however, compositors around the world were setting his name in headlines for the last time. He had made his final mercurial escape—from melancholy, from his dread of invalidism. He was 56.

DOUGLAS FAIRBANKS DEAD

EVENING STANDARD

The funeral, of course, was at Forest Lawn, in the Wee Kirk O' the Heather. Tom Mix attended (right) in his black cowboy suit. Mary Pickford was in Chicago, accompanying her band-leader husband on one of his gigs. But she said as well as anybody what was on everyone's mind: "He passed from our mortal life quickly and spontaneously as he did everything in life, but it is impossible to believe that vibrant and gay spirit could ever perish." Correctly, she was recalling not the man he had become, but the image he had once projected. And, indeed, it was that image that strangers mourned, that image, finally, that was what he wished he were—entirely ageless.

The widow is assisted from the ceremonies by Douglas, Jr. and her sister, Mrs. Basil Bleck. Mary Lee Fairbanks follows.

In character, Charles Chaplin—silent and alone—eloquently expresses his emotions at his old, best friend's passing.

His Own Man

1017-183

Careers perforce proceed, whatever personal sorrows one must absorb. *Green Hell* with Joan Bennett (opposite) had exotic décor, a silly script, and was named 1940's worst by editors of the Harvard *Lampoon* in their annual anti-Hollywood revels. Douglas, Jr. co-produced *Angels Over Broadway,* co-starring Rita Hayworth (right), with Ben Hecht, who also wrote it and was co-director. The film found critical favor—but best beloved by audiences was Fairbanks' dual role in *The Corsican Brothers* (1941).

His finest hour or, more properly, the beginning of it. With profound ties to Britain, Douglas Fairbanks, Jr. was appalled by the strength of isolationist sentiment in the U.S.—and by its persistence even after Hitler attacked England and France in 1939. The most significant of his innumerable contributions to building interventionist sentiment was his vice-chairmanship of The Committee to Defend America by Aiding the Allies, popularly known as the William Allen White Committee. By publicly taking sides in one of the bitterest political controversies in recent American history, he was putting his career on the line—something only a few stars of his rank were willing to do in those days. The climax of this work came on Sept. 18, 1940, when he was the principal speaker at a White Committee rally in Chicago, the heart of isolationist country. Bomb threats were received, vilification by mail and media reached a new height. And he admits to becoming sick with fear—after the rally.

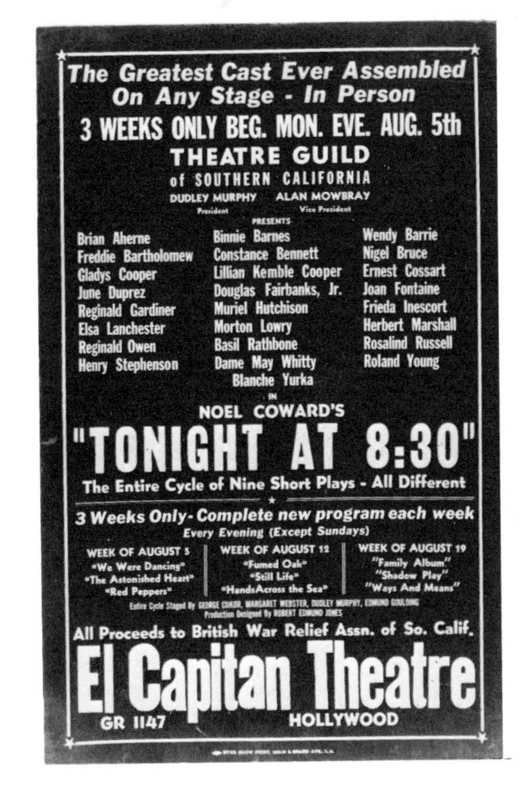

The all-star production of *Tonight at 8:30* raised $60,000 for British relief. By this time Fairbanks was in need of relief himself, his political work, conducted at the expense of paid employment, having put him in debt. And now he had a family to support—his first daughter, Daphne, having been born in April 1940. Below, she celebrates her first Christmas.

(continued)

BRAZIL'S PRESIDENT GETULIO VARGAS HAS FUN WITH U. S. ENVOY EXTRAORDINARY DOUGLAS FAIRBANKS JR. AT A LUNCHEON HELD IN THEIR HONOR IN RIO DE JANEIRO

FAIRBANKS STREWS GOOD WILL THROUGH SOUTH AMERICA

South Americans turned out last week to glimpse an envoy extraordinary of good neighborliness from Washington and Hollywood. Dispatched by President Roosevelt on a 12,000-mile tour to "foster inter-American understanding through the theatrical arts," Douglas Fairbanks Jr. landed in Rio de Janeiro April 25, in Buenos Aires May 12. To State Department officials and others, it may have seemed that the President had picked an extraordinary envoy. But Mickey Rooney wowed Mexico not long ago. South Americans were nearly as enthusiastic about Mr. Fairbanks.

In Rio, President Vargas gave him an hour-long interview. Brazilian society lionized him. At a football game 50,000 fans stood and cheered when he entered the field. Argentines gave him a somewhat less ecstatic reception. The only discordant notes were sounded by Nazi publications. *Pampero*, German propaganda sheet, called him a "spy extraordinary" and promised to return his visit with an Argentine radio crooner named Antonio Caggiano "who is among the worst we have in our country." When a firecracker exploded near Mr. Fairbanks as he entered a broadcasting station, *Pampero* reported the incident under the headline: "Hero of a Hundred Films Almost Dies of Fright." Everywhere he went he was escorted by vigilant U. S. diplomatic attachés, who saw that he met the proper people, said the right things. To date, it is reported, he has pulled no boners.

AMBASSADOR FAIRBANKS RIDES A WATER BIKE IN BRAZIL

On Corcovado Peak, Douglas Fairbanks Jr. and his wife, the former Mrs. G. Huntington Hartford, survey Rio de Janeiro's famed harbor. Monolith of Sugar Loaf Hill rises in left background.

A day in the country outside Rio breaks Fairbanks' routine. At left: Edward Robbins of the Rockefeller Committee, second cousin of President Roosevelt; Mrs. Robbins, Mrs. Fairbanks.

Connections: Fairbanks received a Naval Reserve commission in April 1941, was called to active duty that summer. Above, he reports to Boston Navy Yard, where his friend FDR, Jr. greeted him. They had played together as children in Central Park, had been reunited when Fairbanks became a regular visitor to the White House during the pre-war years. Some months earlier, Fairbanks had undertaken the "good will" mission snidely reported by *Life* opposite. No one knew it was actually a cover for him to gather intelligence on Nazi activity in South America. Less onerous public duties in these years included greeting Elsie Janis—at whose home his father met Mary Pickford—at an Aid-the-Allies party and buying a bauble at a British relief bazaar. The salesperson was Lady Charles Cavendish, John and Robert Kennedy's sister, who died tragically in an airplane crash in 1948.

For Douglas Fairbanks, Jr. there could be no such thing as a phony war. It was a cause in which he deeply believed—and it was also a chance to prove to any remaining doubters that he was something more than just his father's son. His first significant sea duty was aboard the U.S.S. *Mississippi*, shown left, hull down in a North Atlantic gale. Above, in calmer seas off Iceland, Fairbanks posed confidently against background provided by another ship in the convoy headed for Britain.

Detached duty: Fairbanks was assigned to the U.S.S. *Wasp* as a special observer when the American ship was detailed to deliver Spitfires to Malta, where, it is thought, their presence turned the tide in battle for that strategic island. Left, one of the great fighters takes off. Right, Fairbanks chats with an American rating; below he is seen with flying officers.

George R.

Left, the scene is Scapa Flow and His Majesty is inspecting the U.S.S. *Washington*. What he's saying to the Lt. (j.g.) is: "Well, what are you doing here? I haven't seen you since we played golf at Sunningdale before the war." Above, the 1943 Sicilian landings. By this time Fairbanks had acquired his specialty—small boat operations—and he was the planner and often executor of diversionary raids, designed to disguise Allied intentions as to where the main landings in Italy and elsewhere would take place. Novelist John Steinbeck accompanied him (as a war correspondent) on one of these sorties (right), and the Navy thought well enough of Fairbanks' work (a) to have the action recorded by an official Navy artist and (b) to award him the decoration mentioned in Dickie's cable (below).

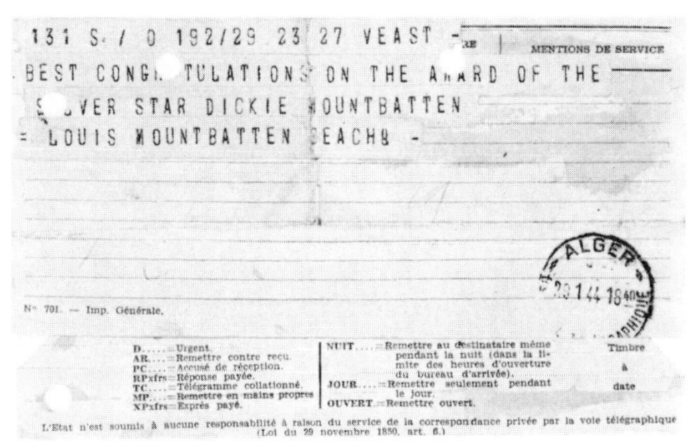

131 S / 0 192/29 23 27 VEAST -

MENTIONS DE SERVICE

BEST CONGR TULATIONS ON THE AWARD OF THE
SILVER STAR DICKIE MOUNTBATTEN
= LOUIS MOUNTBATTEN SEACHQ -

ALGER 29 1 44 18 40 TELEGRAPHIQUE

N° 701. — Imp. Générale.

D.....=Urgent.
AR....=Remettre contre reçu.
PC....=Accusé de réception.
RPxfrs=Réponse payée.
TC....=Télégramme collationné.
MP....=Remettre en mains propres
XPxfrs=Exprès payé.

NUIT....=Remettre au destinataire même pendant la nuit (dans la limite des heures d'ouverture du bureau d'arrivée).
JOUR....=Remettre seulement pendant le jour.
OUVERT.=Remettre ouvert.

Timbre à date

L'Etat n'est soumis à aucune responsabilité à raison du service de la correspondance privée par la voie télégraphique (Loi du 29 novembre 1850, art. 6.)

Fairbanks and his small-boat crews fought off—and sometimes in—Yugoslavia (above), participated in the landings on Elba, then moved on to the South of France where the "Beach Jumpers" (as they were called) staged more diversionary raids. In command of a force of sixteen ships, Fairbanks put troops ashore between Nice and Cannes (drawings at right), then carried out more raids at the Baie de La Ciotat, on the other flank of the main Allied invasion forces. There they were surprised by two German corvettes. Fairbanks, going to the rescue of a crippled landing ship, found himself in a gun duel. He laid down a smoke screen and emerged in a superior position where, despite disabled batteries and damaged engines, he scored the first crippling hit on one of his antagonists and remained in the fight until both were sunk. Below, right, his shipmates. Opposite, on the morning after the battle he leans against one of his damaged turrets, expended shell casings to his right. For this action he received, as the citation indicates, the Legion of Merit with bronze "V" for Valor.

UNITED STATES EIGHTH FLEET

AWARD

The Commander United States EIGHTH Fleet, in the Name of the President of the United States, awards the Legion of Merit to

LIEUTENANT COMMANDER DOUGLAS E. FAIRBANKS, JR., U. S. NAVAL RESERVE

CITATION

For exceptionally meritorious conduct in the performance of outstanding services as Special Operations Planning Officer on the staff of a major Naval Task Force Commander and as Commander of a Naval Task Unit prior to and during the emphibious invasion of Southern France in August 1944.

Lieutenant Commander Fairbanks skillfully and untiringly participated in the development and coordination of plans for the execution of special operations in support of the main Allied landings. In command of a Task Unit, he successfully carried out his mission to establish special assault troops on the flank of the major assault area for the purpose of immobilizing enemy reinforcements attempting to resist the main landings. On the morning of 17 August 1944, he led the ships of his Task Unit into action against two enemy vessels of superior fire power which were attacking a group of smaller craft. By expert and aggressive tactics against heavy odds, he succeeded in containing the enemy until supported by other units of the task group at which time the engagement was again resumed and conducted with great intensity and effectiveness until both enemy ships were sunk by gunfire.

The professional skill, resourcefulness and outstanding devotion to duty displayed by Lieutenant Commander Fairbanks reflected great credit upon himself and the Naval Service.

/s/ H. K. Hewitt

H. K. HEWITT

CONFIDENTIAL

(c) On the night of Dplus one Day, he sailed with the Gunboats and MLs, but minus the PTs, as planned, and bombarded the enemy shore in support of the big diversionary raid in the Baie de la Ciotat with success. Despite heavy return fire by large and medium calibre coastal guns he maneuvered close inshore, through waters known to be mined, and, according to plan, withdrew the next morning at 0440, 17 August.

(d) On receiving a call at 0540 from a disabled ASRC of the Group that it was under attack by two enemy ships, Lt. Commander Fairbanks immediately returned his unit to the area and first engaged the enemy at 10000 yards, opening fire at 0610. Ordering the MLs to screen the Gunboats to seaward, he closed the range to less than 4000 yards while the enemy fire became increasingly accurate and intense. It was then seen that the enemy forces were two Destroyer-Corvette type ships, one a former Italian vessel and the other a large converted yacht, each mounting three radar-controlled 4.7 inch guns and capable of at least 30 knots. Finally, with electric power gone, radio antenna shot away, with some of his main batteries temporarily immobilized by heat and age, his own maximum speed limited to 11 knots, and German shells continually straddling and near-missing his ships, he successfully deployed the unit behind a smoke screen and emerged in a new, tactically superior position as USS Endicott returned, in answer to radio calls, to the scene of action. As the units under Lt. Commander Fairbanks once more closed with the enemy, he succeeded in directing the scoring of the first direct crippling hit on the superior Germans and prevented their retreat. After more intense exchange of fire, and at 0740, both enemy ships had been sunk.

(e) Approximately forty-five of the enemy were killed and one hundred and twenty survivors taken prisoner. The survivors were rescued by ships of the Group and all units withdrew. Minor shrapnel and blast damage were sustained by the Allied ships and there were no fatal casualties to Allied personnel.

(f) The success of the operation, as judged by subsequent intelligence reports, was, to a considerable degree, due to the conception and thorough development of the special plans, produced and, to a considerable extent, executed, with considerable heroism, by Lt. Commander Fairbanks.

H. C. Johnson
Captain, U. S. Navy.

-3-

CLASS OF SERVICE

This is a full-rate Telegram or Cablegram unless its deferred character is indicated by a suitable symbol above or preceding the address.

WESTERN UNION

1201

A. N. WILLIAMS
PRESIDENT

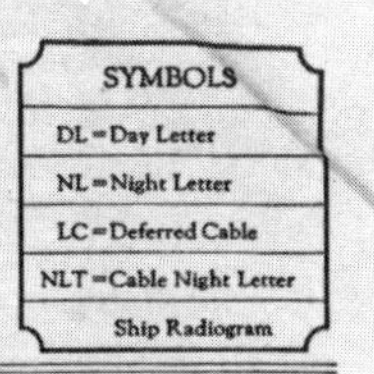

SYMBOLS
DL = Day Letter
NL = Night Letter
LC = Deferred Cable
NLT = Cable Night Letter
Ship Radiogram

The filing time shown in the date line on telegrams and day letters is STANDARD TIME at point of origin. Time of receipt is STANDARD TIME at point of destination

WP132 33 3 EXTRA=CD WINDSOR 16 VIA HOT SPRINGS VIR 19
NLT DOUGLAS FAIRBANKS=
DLR 2228 MASS AVE WASHINGTONDC=
1945 FEB 19 PM 4 58

RETURNED YESTERDAY FROM CONTINENT JUST HEARD ABOUT YOUR BRITISH DECORATION WELL DONE DEAR CHUM STOP SUGGEST THAT IS ENOUGH THIS CAN BE OVERDONE MY FAMILY SENDS ALL LOVE TO YOURS=
DAVID NIVEN.

THE COMPANY WILL APPRECIATE SUGGESTIONS FROM ITS PATRONS CONCERNING ITS SERVICE

Home leave. Mary Lee, Daphne, and newish arrival, Victoria, greet the returning sailor at Norfolk. The telegram from cheeky chum Niven refers to the British Distinguished Service Cross which his Mediterranean exploits earned Fairbanks. He also holds the French Croix de Guerre.

Among the first to go, Fairbanks was among the last movie stars to return. It was 1946 before he was mustered out and came home to Hollywood to greet his stepmother.

Back home, he sharpened up old skills (left) and renewed membership in the "Cad's Club" (below). A partial membership roster included David Niven, Rex Harrison, and Robert Coote. Their motto was "Everything Rampant, Anything Couchant." Opposite, Fairbanks re-established himself with a film in his father's old vein, *Sinbad the Sailor* (1947), which surprised him by being commercially more successful than he had dared hope.

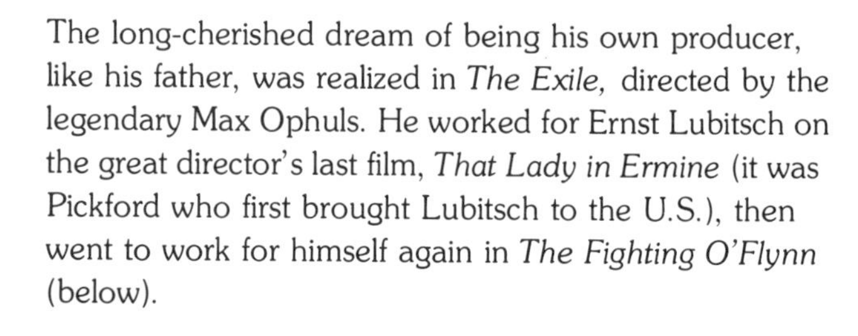

The long-cherished dream of being his own producer, like his father, was realized in *The Exile,* directed by the legendary Max Ophuls. He worked for Ernst Lubitsch on the great director's last film, *That Lady in Ermine* (it was Pickford who first brought Lubitsch to the U.S.), then went to work for himself again in *The Fighting O'Flynn* (below).

1582-162

D. V. M.

Congratulation Daddy.
For your Knighthood today
with H.M. the King.
We will never forget july 12, 1949
will we??? ✧✧✧ and this goes for
D. V. M. D. V. M.
Lady Fairbanks too.
Love, Love, Love.
Daphne
Victoria
Melissa
G.W.

News of Fairbanks' knighthood, awarded for his efforts to foster friendship between the U.S. and Britain, was received in Los Angeles in the spring of 1949, but he was on his way to England anyway and was able to receive it from his old friend from Scapa Flow personally. The children marked the day with a note and he and Mary Lee were photographed outside Buckingham Palace (right) after the award was made.

Fairbanks' next-to-last feature was among the best films he ever made. Known in England as *State Secret* and in the U.S. as *The Great Manhunt,* it was a tough, tense blend of cold-war politics and espionage, co-starring Glynis Johns, Jack Hawkins and Herbert Lom, shot on location in the Dolomites. It was not, however, the sort of "big" picture the industry was banking on to compete with television—where everything was little—in 1950. Shortly thereafter, feeling that if he could not lick TV he might as well join it, Fairbanks began producing, hosting (and starring in every fourth episode of) "Douglas Fairbanks Presents," an anthology series that ran for five seasons.

The producer in action (above) on the sound stage at Elstree. In a typical week he would have two half-hour shows (on five-day schedules) going simultaneously. Despite tight budgets—less than $30,000 per show—he felt the overall quality of the series was high and remains especially proud of the caliber of actors he was able to recruit. Left, top to bottom, some typical programs: *Runaway Marriage, Four Farewells, International Settlement.* Opposite, he maintains his dignity while all about him are losing theirs in a guest appearance on somebody-or-other's television program.

SALOON

Many of the decorations Fairbanks wears in the formal portrait taken just before the coronation in 1952 (opposite) were for his international charitable work. Among the most significant of his activities in this field was his chairmanship of the Share through CARE program, a fund-raising operation. Above, he distributes food packages in Holland. Left, he greets the Queen at the U.S. booth at the 1948 "Thank You" exhibition (for food gifts) in London. With them are Sharman Douglas and her mother, daughter and wife of U.S. Ambassador to the Court of St. James's.

Armstrong Jones

Insiders: With friends at court, the Fairbanks family was able to obtain a privileged position from which to view the changing of the guard in the early fifties, the *pater familias* maintaining admirable cool over the whole business (below). The Queen herself took dinner at the Fairbankses on one highly publicized occasion (and several that were less so), was once glimpsed on television presiding over an outdoor barbecue outfit Douglas had presented her. Right, other establishment figures found the company of the Fairbankses easy. In the top photo, right, the Dowager Queen Mary was snapped by Douglas with, left to right, H.R.H. Prince Michael of Kent, H.R.H. Princess Marina, Duchess of Kent, Daphne and Victoria Fairbanks, H.R.H. Princess Alexandra of Kent, Melissa and Mary Lee Fairbanks. Center, Anthony Eden takes his ease at the Fairbanks' weekend place at Bogner Regis in 1952, and bottom, Douglas, despite an abcessed tooth, joins Harold Macmillan on a shoot at Tillypronie, in Scotland.

For almost a quarter century the Fairbanks' home in London—they also maintain addresses in Palm Beach and New York—has been The Boltons, a shallow ellipse of grass and plane trees not far from Chelsea. The homes there were all built by a developer in late Victorian days, handsome and solid, and the atmosphere is of a private enclave, isolated from the city's bustle. The interior reflects Mary Lee Fairbanks' superb taste in antiques, her husband's concern for preserving and displaying mementos of his own, his family's, past.

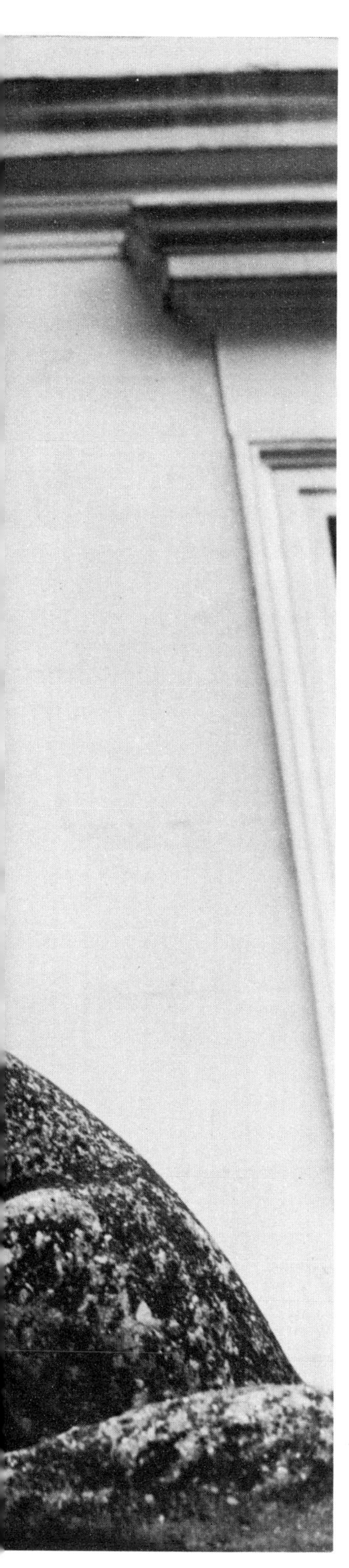

The first published photo by a young photographer's assistant (right) was of Melissa Fairbanks and it appeared—its subject unidentified—in *The Tatler.* Until he grew more famous for other reasons, he frequently recorded the family's important occasions and, more than once, did its Christmas card.

INSURANCE
It was a great occasion!
Kindest regards to Douglas Fairbanks, Jr. Harry Truman

Senior's 1918 postcard from the Executive Suite seems prophetic, for over the past five decades his son has been a frequent caller at the White House, in semi-official capacities as well as glamourous dinner guest. A great admirer of Harry Truman (opposite, an underground conference), Fairbanks served in his administration as part-time consultant. Top, with Betty Ford while in Washington preparing *Present Laughter* in 1975. In addition to maintaining political interests, he remained active in the Naval Reserve long after the war. Retiring from the Active Reserve in 1969, he returned temporarily to duty to serve as U.S. Naval Delegate to the SEATO Conference. Above, a cheerful Captain Fairbanks departs a ship of the Sixth Fleet on NATO exercises.

Douglas Fairbanks appears to have no former friends. Below, he poses with Dolores Del Rio. Right, he meets Merle Oberon in Acapulco. Bottom, he is out of the picture (though Mary Lee is in it at left) during a South-of-France visit with the oldest of old family friends.

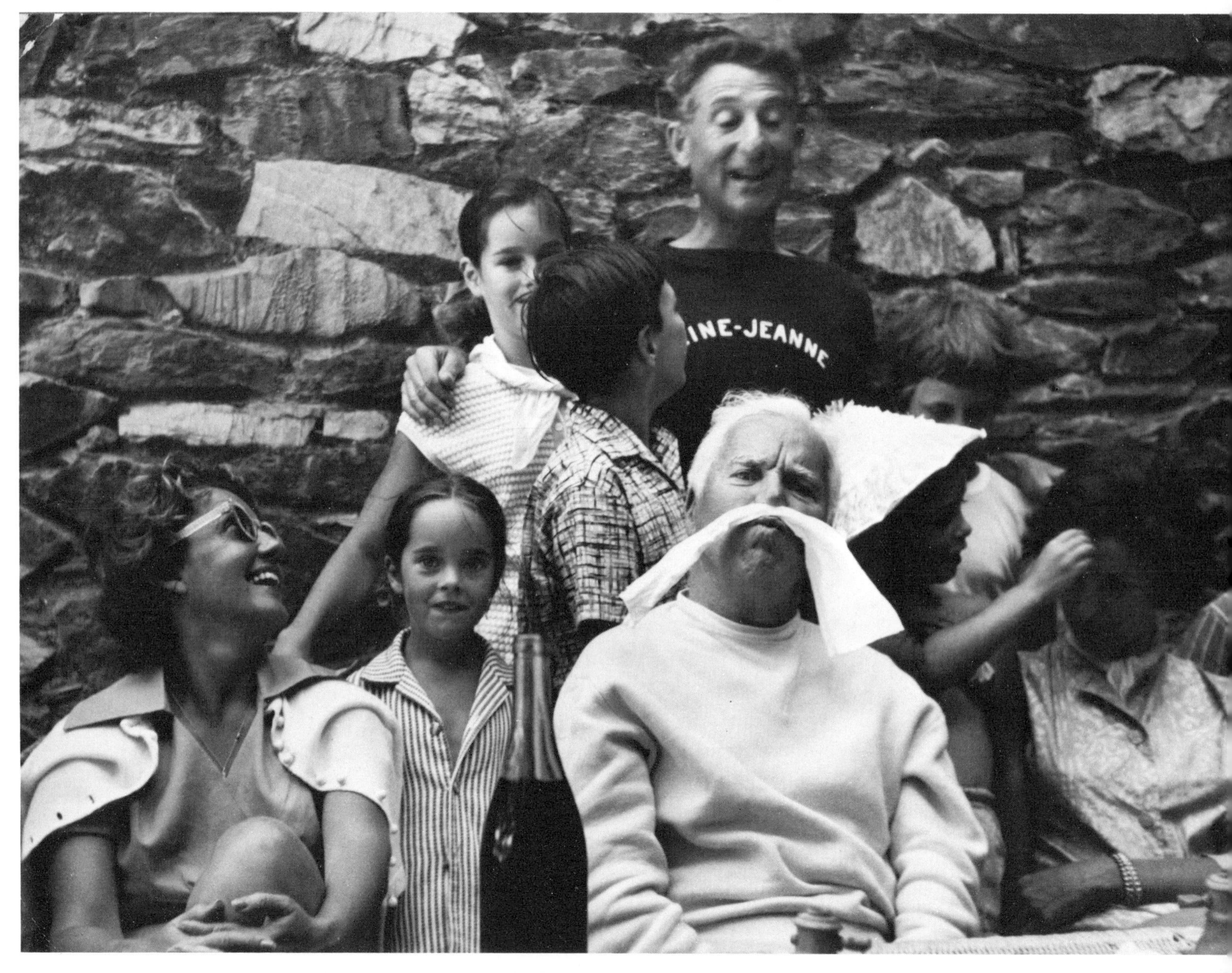

Left, a formal occasion—Fairbanks and "Dickie" Mountbatten receive perhaps superfluous decorations from the VFW—of small concern to the man in the background, who has everything. Below, the Admiral of the Fleet is not seasick, just utterly relaxed on a Mexican fishing trip.

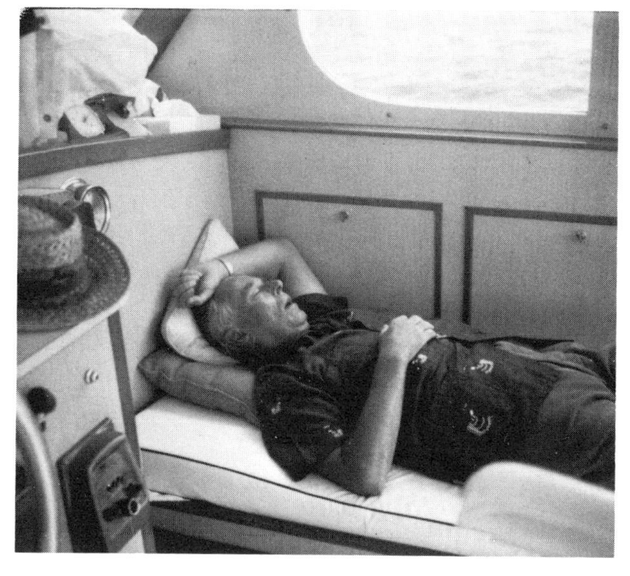

Left, another old friend—and co-star—joins Mary Lee on a Barbados vacation. Greta Garbo obviously has no fear of Douglas Fairbanks' camera.

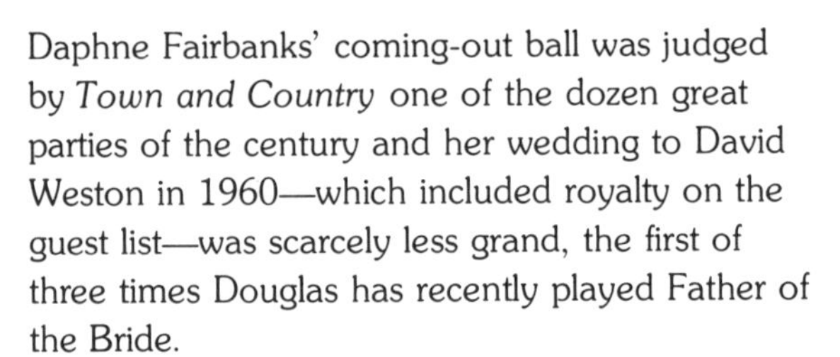

Daphne Fairbanks' coming-out ball was judged by *Town and Country* one of the dozen great parties of the century and her wedding to David Weston in 1960—which included royalty on the guest list—was scarcely less grand, the first of three times Douglas has recently played Father of the Bride.

A study in contrasts: Douglas Fairbanks, Jr. is distinctly not himself in a musical version of *Tom Jones* for Canadian television.

As an actor, Douglas Fairbanks has worked mostly on the stage in recent years, and one of his triumphs was in the West Coast revival of *My Fair Lady* in 1969. He brought along the portrait of Shaw as a dressing room decoration and is pointing it out to adapters Lerner and Lowe in the photograph above. Opposite, "The Rain in Spain" becomes a torrent of joy for Prof. Higgins.

to Douglas Fairbanks the Second
from one who remembers the First
G Bernard Shaw
9th August 1947

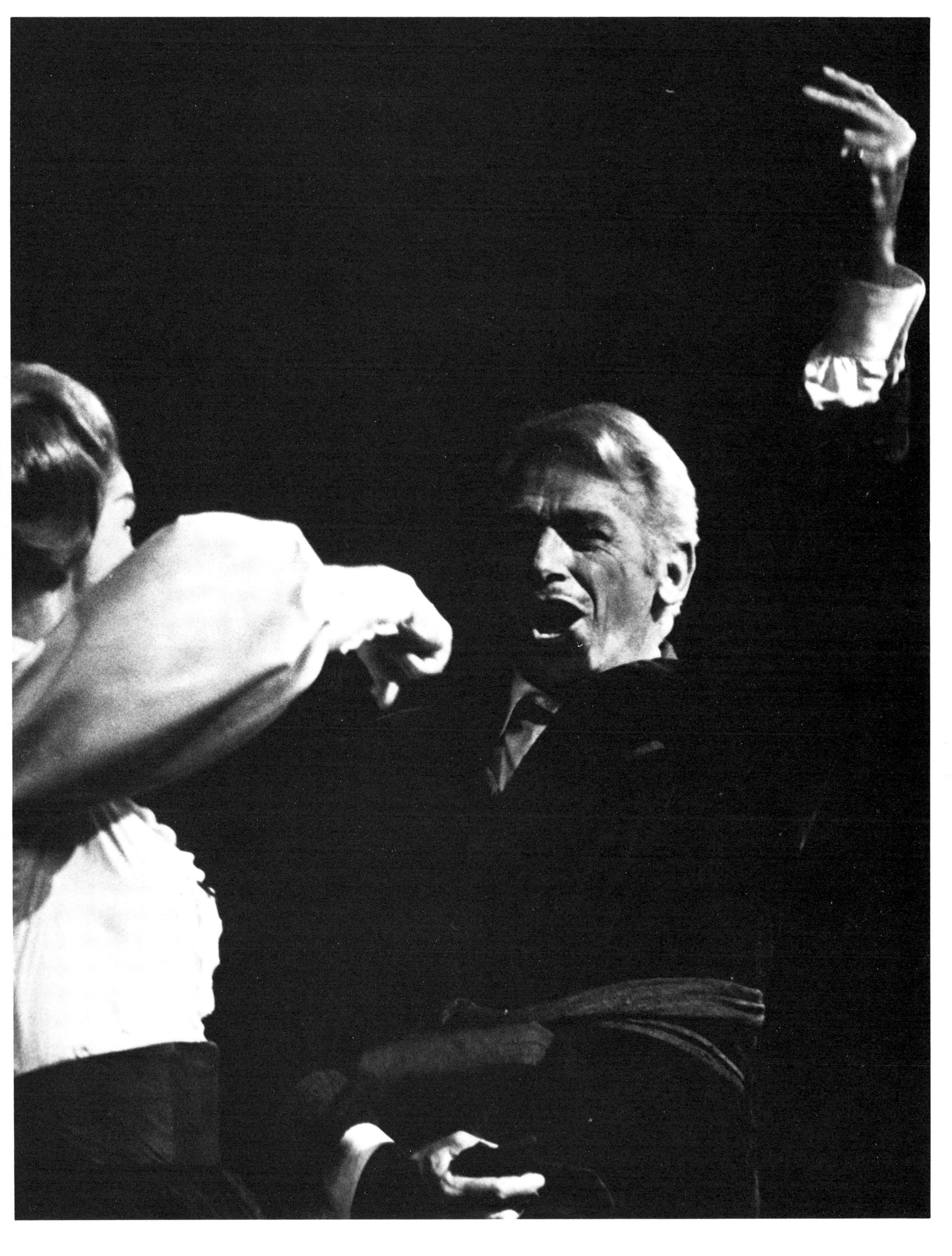

Traditions carried on: Above, Fairbanks introduces American television audiences to "Moss Bros.," the legendary purveyors of rental finery for any and all English ceremonies and occasions. The program was a special broadcast on the eve of Princess Anne's wedding. Right, the daughter of one great theatrical house—Vanessa Redgrave—joins the son of another for the "Red and Blue" segment (directed by Tony Richardson) of a 1968 trilogy intended for theatrical release, but which found few theaters interested.

A family portrait. In the top row, Barend and Victoria Van Gerbig, David and Daphne Weston, Richard and Melissa Morant; in front of them, Barend, Jr. and Eliza Van Gerbig, Natasha, Anthony, Nicholas, and Dominick Weston. Richard Morant—known to television audiences as Flashman in *Tom Brown's School Days*—holds baby Crystal, while his son, Joseph, a/k/a "The Bruiser," strikes off on his own.

The Pleasure of His Company: David Niven and Cary Grant join Fairbanks at a charity function in Leeds in 1974, the same year Fairbanks, lithe and blithe as ever, revived the play of the same name—and one of his favorite vehicles—in Toronto.

CHRONOLOGY Douglas Fairbanks, Sr.

Note: The authors and editors are grateful to Eileen Bowser and Robert Regan of the Department of Film, The Museum of Modern Art, for their help in updating this chronology, which first appeared in Alistair Cooke, *Douglas Fairbanks: The Making of a Screen Character* (copyright ©1940, The Museum of Modern Art, New York. All rights reserved).

1883 May 23 Born Denver, Colo., Douglas Elton Ulman, son of H. Charles Ulman and Ella Adelaide (Marsh).

1888-99 Attended Jarvis Military Academy, East Denver High School, Colorado School of Mines.

1900 Sept. 10 First professional stage appearance as Florio in *The Duke's Jester* at the Academy of Music in Richmond, Va.

1902 Feb. 24 First Broadway appearance as Glen Masters in *Her Lord and Master* at the Manhattan Theatre.

1903 National tour in *Mrs. Jack.*

1904 Feb. Landry Court in *The Pit.*

1904-07 *Two Little Sailor Boys, Fanata, Frenzied Finance, Clothes, As Ye Sow, The Man of the Hour.*

1907 July 11 Married Anna Beth Sully, daughter of Daniel J. Sully, in Providence, R.I.

1908 Aug. *All for a Girl.*

1909 Dec. 9 Douglas Fairbanks, Jr. born in New York City.

1909-11 National tour as Bud Haines in *A Gentleman from Mississippi.*

1911-12 In vaudeville with act called *A Regular Business Man.*

1912-14 On Broadway as lead in *Officer 666, Hawthome of the U.S.A., The Show Shop*

1915 Signed by Harry Aitken of Triangle Film Corporation and went to Hollywood.

THE LAMB. Sept. 23. Dir. by W. Christy Cabanne, supervised by D. W. Griffith. Script by Cabanne, from a story by Griffith. With Seena Owen.

DOUBLE TROUBLE. Dec. 5. Dir. by W. Christy Cabanne, supervised by D. W. Griffith. Script by Griffith and Cabanne, from a novel by Herbert Quick. With Margery Wilson.

1916 HIS PICTURE IN THE PAPERS. Feb. 10. Dir. by John Emerson, supervised by D. W. Griffith. Script by Anita Loos. With Loretta Blake.

THE HABIT OF HAPPINESS. March 12. Dir. by Allan Dwan, supervised by D. W. Griffith. Script by Shannon Fife and Dwan, from an idea by Griffith. With Dorothy West.

THE GOOD BAD MAN. April 13. Dir. by Allan Dwan, supervised by D. W. Griffith. Script by Fairbanks. With Bessie Love.

REGGIE MIXES IN. May 28. Dir. by W. Christy Cabanne, supervised by D. W. Griffith. Script by Roy Somerville. With Bessie Love.

THE MYSTERY OF THE LEAPING FISH. June 11. Dir. by John Emerson, supervised by D. W. Griffith. Script by Tod Browning. With Bessie Love, Alma Rubens.

FLIRTING WITH FATE. June 25. Dir. by W. Christy Cabanne, supervised by D. W. Griffith. Script by Cabanne, from a story by Robert M. Baker. With Jewel Carmen.

THE HALF-BREED. July 9. Dir. By Allan Dwan, supervised by D. W. Griffith. Script by Anita Loos, from a story by Bret Harte. With Alma Rubens, Jewel Carmen. Reissued as *Flames of '49.*

MANHATTAN MADNESS. Sept. 10. Dir. by Allan Dwan, supervised by D. W. Griffith. Script by E.V. Durling. With Jewel Carmen.

AMERICAN ARISTOCRACY. Nov. 5. Dir. by Lloyd Ingraham, supervised by D. W. Griffith. Script by Anita Loos. With Jewel Carmen, Albert Parker.

THE MATRIMANIAC. Dec. 3. Dir. by Paul Powell, supervised by D. W. Griffith. Script by Anita Loos and John Emerson, from a story by Octavus Roy Cohen and J. V. Glesy. With Constance Talmadge.

THE AMERICANO. Dec. 24. Dir. by John Emerson, supervised by D. W. Griffith. Script by Anita Loos and Emerson, from a novel by Eugene P. Lyle, Jr. With Alma Rubens. Remade in 1925 as *American Pluck.*

Dec. Set up the Douglas Fairbanks Film Corporation, to release through the Famous Players-Lasky Film Corporation.

1917 IN AGAIN—OUT AGAIN. April 22. Dir. by John Emerson. Script by Anita Loos. With Arline Pretty, Bull Montana, Albert Parker.

WILD AND WOOLY. July 5. Dir. by John Emerson. Script by Anita Loos, from a story by Horace B. Carpenter. With Eileen Percy, Sam de Grasse.

DOWN TO EARTH. Aug. 12. Dir. by John Emerson. Script by Anita Loos, from a story by Fairbanks. With Eileen Percy, Gustav von Seyffertitz.

THE MAN FROM PAINTED POST. Sept. 30. Dir. by Joseph Henabery. Script by Fairbanks, from a story by Jackson Gregory. With Eileen Percy, Frank Campeau.

REACHING FOR THE MOON. Nov. 18. Dir. by John Emerson. Script by Anita Loos and Emerson. With Eileen Percy, Eugene Ormonde, Frank Campeau, Erich von Stroheim.

1918 A MODERN MUSKETEER. Jan. 3. Dir. by Allan Dwan. Script by Dwan, from a novel by Eugene P. Lyle, Jr. With Marjorie Daw, Frank Campeau, ZaSu Pitts.

HEADIN' SOUTH. March 18. Dir. by Arthur Rosson,

supervised by Allan Dwan. Script by Allan Dwan. With Katherine MacDonald, Frank Campeau.

MR. FIX-IT. April 5. Dir. by Allan Dwan. Script by Dwan, from a story by Ernest Butterworth. With Marjorie Daw, Katherine MacDonald, Frank Campeau.

SAY! YOUNG FELLOW. June 16. Dir. by Joseph Henabery. Script by Henabery. With Marjorie Daw, Frank Campeau.

BOUND IN MOROCCO. July 28. Dir. by Allan Dwan. Script by Dwan. With Pauline Curley, Edythe Chapman, Frank Campeau.

HE COMES UP SMILING. Sept. 8. Dir. by Allan Dwan. Script by Frances Marion, from a novel by Charles Sherman and a play by Byron Ongley. With Marjorie Daw, Bull Montana, Frank Campeau.

Nov. 30 Beth Sully Fairbanks received divorce and custody of Douglas, Jr., White Plains, N.Y.

ARIZONA. Dec. 8. Dir. by Fairbanks. Script by Fairbanks, from a play by Augustus Thomas. With Marjorie Daw, Marguerite de la Motte, Frank Campeau.

1919 Feb. 5 Formed United Artists with D. W. Griffith, Charles Chaplin, and Mary Pickford.

THE KNICKERBOCKER BUCKAROO. May 25. Dir. by Albert Parker. Script by Fairbanks. With Marjorie Daw, William Wellman, Frank Campeau. Final Artcraft release.

HIS MAJESTY, THE AMERICAN. Sept. 27. Dir. by Joseph Henabery. Script by Henabery and Elton Banks [Fairbanks]. With Marjorie Daw, Frank Campeau, Boris Karloff.

WHEN THE CLOUDS ROLL BY. Dec. 28. Dir. by Victor Fleming. Script by Fairbanks, Lewis Weadon, and Tom J. Geraghty. With Kathleen Clifford, Frank Campeau.

1920 March 28 Married Gladys Smith (Mary Pickford) in Hollywood.

THE MOLLYCODDLE. June 13. Dir. by Victor Fleming. Script by Tom J. Geraghty and Fairbanks, from a story by Harold McGrath. With Ruth Renick, Betty Boulton, Wallace Beery and, as extras, Mary Pickford and Charles Chaplin.

THE MARK OF ZORRO. Nov. 28. Dir. by Fred Niblo. Script by Elton Thomas [Fairbanks], from a novel by Johnston McCulley. With Marguerite de la Motte, Noah Beery.

1921 THE NUT. March 19. Dir. by Ted Reed. Script by Elton Thomas [Fairbanks], from a story by Kenneth Davenport. With Marguerite de la Motte, Barbara LaMarr and, as himself, Charles Chaplin.

THE THREE MUSKETEERS. Aug. 28. Dir. by Fred Niblo. Script by Edward Knoblock, Elton Thomas [Fairbanks], and Lotta Woods, from a novel by Alexandre Dumas. With Marguerite de la Motte, Barbara LaMarr, Adolphe Menjou.

1922 ROBIN HOOD. Oct. 18. Dir. by Allan Dwan. Script by Elton Thomas [Fairbanks] and Lotta Woods. With Enid Bennett, Wallace Beery and, as an extra, Mary Pickford.

1924 THE THIEF OF BAGDAD. March 18. Dir. by Raoul Walsh. Script by Elton Thomas [Fairbanks] and Lotta Woods. With Julanne Johnston, Anna May Wong, Noble Johnson.

1925 DON Q, SON OF ZORRO. June 15. Dir. by Donald Crisp. Script by Jack Cunningham, from a novel by K. and Hesketh Prichard. With Mary Astor, Donald Crisp, Warner Oland, Jean Hersholt, Lottie Pickford Forrest.

1926 THE BLACK PIRATE. March 8. Dir. by Albert Parker. Script by Jack Cunningham and Lotta Woods, from a story by Elton Thomas [Fairbanks]. With Billie Dove, Donald Crisp. Photographed in Technicolor.

1927 THE GAUCHO. Nov. 21. Dir. by F. Richard Jones. Script by Elton Thomas [Fairbanks]. With Lupe Velez, Eve Southern, Gustav von Seyffertitz and, as Our Lady of the Miracle, Mary Pickford.

1929 THE IRON MASK. Feb. 21. Dir. by Allan Dwan. Script by Elton Thomas [Fairbanks], from novels by Alexandre Dumas and memoirs by D'Artagnan, Richelieu, and de Rochefort. With Marguerite de la Motte, Belle Bennett, and Dorothy Revier. Originally shown with spoken prologue and epilogue by Fairbanks.

THE TAMING OF THE SHREW. Oct. 26. Full sound. Dir. by Sam Taylor. Script by Taylor, from the play by William Shakespeare. With Mary Pickford, Clyde Cook, and Dorothy Jordan. All talking.

1930 REACHING FOR THE MOON. Dec. 29. Dir. by Edmund Goulding. Script by Goulding, from a story by Irving Berlin. With Bebe Daniels, Edward Everett Horton, Bing Crosby.

1931 AROUND THE WORLD IN 80 MINUTES. Nov. 10. Dir. by Victor Fleming and Fairbanks. Script by Fairbanks and Robert E. Sherwood. A travelogue with Fairbanks, Fleming, the crew, and celebrities of foreign lands.

1932 March Sailed from San Francisco for Tahiti.

MR. ROBINSON CRUSOE. Aug. 19. Dir. by Edward Sutherland. Script by Tom Geraghty, from a story by Elton Thomas [Fairbanks]. With Maria Alba, William Farnum.

August Sailed from San Francisco for game hunt in the Orient. Returned through Siberia to Paris, arriving in New York Dec. 20.

1934 THE PRIVATE LIFE OF DON JUAN. Nov. 30. Dir. by Alexander Korda. Script by Frederick Lonsdale, Lajos Biro. With Merle Oberon, Benita Hume, Binnie Barnes, Gibson Gowland. Made in England for London Films.

1936 Jan. 10 Divorced by Mary Pickford.

March 7 Married the former Lady Sylvia Ashley in Paris.

1938 Dec. 7 Formed production company, Fairbanks-International.

1939 Dec. 12 Died in his sleep at home in Beverly Hills, Calif.

CHRONOLOGY Douglas Fairbanks, Jr.

Compiled by Raymond Rohauer and Anthony Slide.

1909 Dec. 9 Born New York City, son of Douglas Fairbanks, Sr. and Anna Beth Sully.

1916-23 Attended Bovée School and Collegiate School (also Cadet at Knickerbocker Greys), New York City; Pasadena Polytechnic School, Pasadena; and Harvard Military School, Los Angeles. Privately tutored in London and Paris. Also began studies of art and languages at this time.

1923 June 18 Arrived in Los Angeles under contract to Famous Players/Lasky Corp.
STEPHEN STEPS OUT. Famous players/Lasky. Rel. by Paramount, Nov. Dir. by Joseph Henabery. DFJr., Theodore Roberts, Noah Beery, Harry Myers, Fannie Midgley.

1924 After brief return to Paris, settled in Los Angeles with mother and continued film career.

THE AIR MAIL. Famous Players/Lasky. March. Dir. by Irvin Willat. Warner Baxter, Billie Dove, Mary Brian, DFJr.

1925 THE AMERICAN VENUS. Famous Players/Lasky. Jan. 25. Dir. by Frank Tuttle. Esther Ralston, Lawrence Gray, Ford Sterling, Fay Lamphier, Louise Brooks, Edna May Oliver, Kenneth MacKenna, William B. Mack, George DeCarlton, W. T. Benda, Ernest Torrence, DFJr. (who plays Triton in Miss America sequence).
WILD HORSE MESA. Famous Players/Lasky. Sept. 14. Dir. by George B. Seitz. Jack Holt, Noah Beery, Billie Dove, DFJr.
STELLA DALLAS. Samuel Goldwyn, Inc. Nov. Dir. by Henry King. Ronald Colman, Belle Bennett, Alice Joyce, Jean Hersholt, Lois Moran, DFJr.

1926 PADLOCKED. Famous Players/Lasky. Aug. 9. Dir. by Allan Dwan. Lois Moran, Noah Beery, Louise Dresser, Helen Jerome Eddy, DFJr.
BROKEN HEARTS OF HOLLYWOOD. Warner Bros. Aug. 14. Dir. by Lloyd Bacon. Patsy Ruth Miller, Louise Dresser, DFJr., Jerry Miley, Barbara Worth.
MAN BAIT. Metropolitan Pictures. Rel. by P.D.C., Dec. Dir. by Donald Crisp. Marie Prevost, Kenneth Thomson, DFJr., Louis Natheaux, Sally Rand.

1927 WOMEN LOVE DIAMONDS. MGM. Feb. 12. Dir. by Edmund Goulding. Pauline Starke, Owen Moore, Lionel Barrymore, Cissy Fitzgerald, Gwen Lee, DFJr.
IS ZAT SO? Fox Film Corp. May 15. Dir. by Alfred E. Green. With George O'Brien, Edmund Lowe, Kathryn Perry, Cyril Chadwick, Doris Lloyd, Dione Ellis, DFJr.
A TEXAS STEER. Sam E. Rork Prod. Rel. by First National, Dec. 4. Dir. by Richard Wallace. Will Rogers, Louise Fazenda, Sam Hardy, Ann Rork, DFJr.

1927-28 Appeared in John van Druten's *Young Woodley*, Majestic Theater, Los Angeles, and in San Francisco (his third stage appearance; the earlier ones also in 1927). Appeared intermittently on the stage for the next thirteen years between film assignments.

1928 DEAD MAN'S CURVE. FBO Pictures. Jan. 15. Dir. by Richard Rosson. DFJr., Sally Blane, Charles Byer, Arthur Metcalf, Joel McCrae.
MODERN MOTHERS. Columbia. May 13. Dir. by Philip Rosen. Helene Chadwick, DFJr., Ethel Grey Terry, Barbara Kent.
THE TOILERS. Tiffany-Stahl Prod. Oct. 1. Music and sound effects. Dir. by Reginald Barker. DFJr., Jobyna Ralston, Harvey Clark, Wade Boteler, Robert Ryan. One song dubbed for DFJr.
THE POWER OF THE PRESS. Columbia. Oct. 31. Dir. by Frank Capra. DFJr., Jobyna Ralston, Mildred Harris, Philo McCullough, Wheeler Oakman.
A WOMAN OF AFFAIRS. MGM. Dec. 15. Music and sound effects. Dir. by Clarence Brown. Greta Garbo, John Gilbert, Lewis Stone, John Mack Brown, DFJr.
THE BARKER. First National. Dec. 19. Part-talkie. Dir. by George Fitzmaurice. Milton Sills, Dorothy Mackaill, Betty Compson, DFJr., George Cooper, John Erwin.

1929 THE JAZZ AGE. FBO Pictures. Feb. 10. Part-talkie and musical score. Dir. by Lynn Shores. DFJr., Marceline Day, Henry B. Walthall, Myrtle Stedman, Joel McCrea.

June 3 Married Joan Crawford in New York City. (Divorced 1933.)

FAST LIFE. First National. Aug. 15. Full sound. Dir. by John Francis Dillon. DFJr., Loretta Young, William Holden, Chester Morris, Frank Sheridan.
OUR MODERN MAIDENS. MGM. Aug. 24. Sound effects and musical score. Dir. by Jack Conway. Joan Crawford, Rod LaRocque, DFJr., Anita Page, Edward Nugent.
THE CARELESS AGE. First National. Sept. 15. (Full sound, as are all films hereafter.) Dir. by John Griffith Wray. DFJr., Carmel Myers, Holmes Herbert, Kenneth Thompson, Loretta Young, Ilka Chase.
THE FORWARD PASS. First National. Nov. 10. Dir. by Eddie Cline. DFJr., Loretta Young, Guinn Williams, Marion Byron, Phyllis Crane.
THE SHOW OF SHOWS. Warner Bros. Nov. 20. Dir. by John G. Adolfi. A revue with many stars. Master of ceremonies, Frank Fay. Frame story stars William Courtenay, H. B. Warner, Hobart Bosworth, John Barrymore. DFJr. appears in "Bicycle Built for Two" sequence, with Chester Conklin, Lois Wilson, and others.

1930 PARTY GIRL. Victory Pictures. Rel. by Tiffany, Jan. 1. Dir. by Victor Halperin. DFJr., Jeanette Loff, Judith Barrie, Marie Prevost.
LOOSE ANKLES. First National. Feb. Dir. by Ted Wilde. DFJr., Loretta Young, Louise Fazenda, Ethel Wales, Otis Harlan, Daphne Pollard.
DAWN PATROL. First National. July 10. Dir. by Howard Hawks. Richard Barthelmess, Neil Hamilton, DFJr., William Janney, James Finlayson.
THE LITTLE ACCIDENT. Universal. Aug. Dir. by William James Craft. DFJr., Anita Page, Sally Blane, ZaSu Pitts, Roscoe Karns, Slim Summerville.
OUTWARD BOUND. Warner Bros. Rel. by First National, Nov. 29. Dir. by Robert Milton. Leslie Howard, DFJr., Helen Chandler, Beryl Mercer, Alison Skipworth, Montagu Love, Dudley Digges, Lyonel Watts.
THE WAY OF ALL MEN. First National. Sept. 7. Remake of 1922 film, THE SIN FLOOD. Dir. by Frank Lloyd. DFJr., Dorothy Revier, Robert Edeson, Anders Randolf, Noah Beery.
ONE NIGHT AT SUSIE'S. First National. Oct. 19. Dir. by John Francis Dillon. Bille Dove, DFJr., Helen Ware, Tully Marshall, Jame Crane, John Loder.

1931 LITTLE CAESAR. Warner Bros. Rel. by First National, Jan. 25. Dir. by Mervyn LeRoy. Edward G. Robinson, DFJr., Glenda Farrell, Sidney Blackmer, George E. Stone.
CHANCES. Warner Bros. Rel. by First National, July 18. Dir. by Allan Dwan. DFJr., Anthony Bushell, Rose Hobart, Mary Forbestein.

Offically became a star.

I LIKE YOUR NERVE. Warner Bros. Rel. by First National, Sept. 12. Dir. by William McGann. DFJr., Loretta Young, Henry Kolker, Boris Karloff, Claude Allister.
UNION DEPOT. Warner Bros. Rel. by First National, Jan. 30. Dir. by Alfred E. Green. DFJr., Joan Blondell, Guy Kibbee, Alan Hale, Frank McHugh.
IT'S TOUGH TO BE FAMOUS! Warner Bros. Rel. by First National, June 25. Dir. by Alfred E. Green. DFJr., Mary Brian, Lillian Bond, Walter Catlett, Louise Beavers.
LOVE IS A RACKET. Warner Bros. Rel. by First National, June 25. Dir. by William A. Wellman. DFJr., Frances Dee, Lee Tracy, Lyle Talbot, Ann Dvorak.

1932 SCARLET DAWN. Warner Bros. Rel. by First National, Nov. Dir. by William Dieterle. DFJr., Nancy Carroll, Lilyan Tashman, Guy Kibbee.
LE PLOMBIER AMOUREUX. MGM. French version of THE PASSIONATE PLUMBER. Dir. by Claude Autant-Lara. Buster Keaton, Jeanette Ferney, DFJr.
L'ATHLETE MALGRE LUI. Warner Bros. Dir. by William McGann.
L'AVIATEUR. Warner Bros. Dir. by William McGann.

1933 PARACHUTE JUMPER. Warner Bros. Jan. Dir. by Alfred E. Green. DFJr., Bette Davis, Leo Carillo, Frank McHugh, Claire Dodd.
THE LIFE OF JIMMY DOLAN. Warner Bros. June. Dir. by Archie Mayo. DFJr., Loretta Young, Aline MacMahon, Lyle Talbot, Mickey Rooney, John Wayne, Guy Kibbee.
THE NARROW CORNER. Warner Bros. July. Dir. by Alfred E. Green. DFJr., Patricia Ellis, Ralph Bellamy, Dudley Digges, Sidney Toler.
CAPTURED. Warner Bros. Aug. Dir. by Roy Del Ruth. Leslie Howard, DFJr., Paul Lukas, Margaret Lindsay, J. Carroll Naish.
MORNING GLORY. RKO. Aug., Dir. by Lowell Sherman. Katharine Hepburn, DFJr., Adolphe Menjou, Mary Duncan, C. Aubrey Smith.

1934 CATHERINE THE GREAT. London Films, dist. by United Artists. U.S. rel. Feb. Dir. by Paul Czinner. DFJr., Elisabeth Bergner, Flora Robson, Sir Gerald DuMaurier.
SUCCESS AT ANY PRICE (SUCCESS STORY). RKO. May. Dir. by J. Walter Ruben. Colleen Moore, DFJr., Genevieve Tobin, Frank Morgan, Edward Everett Horton, Allen Vincent.

1935 London, established Criterion Films Ltd. (films released through United Artists).

MIMI. B.I.P. (British). Rel. in U.K. by Wardour, May; in U.S. by United Artists, Dec. Dir. by Paul Stein. DFJr., Gertrude Lawrence, Diana Napier, Harold Warrender, Carol Goodner.
MAN OF THE MOMENT. Warner Bros. (British). Sept. Dir. by Monty Banks. DFJr., Laura La Plante, Margaret Lockwood, Claude Hulbert, Donald Calthrop.

1936 THE AMATEUR GENTLEMAN. Criterion Films (Prod. by DFJr. and Marcel Hellman). U.K. rel., Jan.; U.S. rel. by United Artists, April. Dir. by Thornton Freeland. Screenplay by Clemence Dane. DFJr., Elissa Landi, Gordon Harker, Margaret Lockwood, Hugh Williams, Basil Sydney, Irene Brown, Carol Brown, Athol Stewart, Esme Percy.
ACCUSED. Criterion Films (Prod. by DFJr. and Marcel Hellman). U.K. rel., July; U.S. rel. by United Artists, Dec. Dir. by Thornton Freeland. DFJr., Dolores del Rio, Florence Desmond, Basil Sydney, Cecil Humphreys, Esme Percy, Googie Withers, Roland Culver. Leo Genn.

1937 WHEN THIEF MEETS THIEF. Criterion Films (Prod. by DFJr. and Marcel Hellman). U.K. rel. (as JUMP FOR GLORY), March; U.S. rel. by United Artists, June. Dir. by Raoul Walsh. Based on novel, *Jump for Glory*. DFJr., Valerie Hobson, Alan Hale, Jack Melford, Esme Percy, Leo Genn, Basil Radford.

1937-38 First official and semi-official governmental duties assigned by President Roosevelt and Secretary of State Cordell Hull.

THE PRISONER OF ZENDA. Selznick International. Rel. by United Artists Sept. 3. Dir. by John Cromwell. Ronald Colman, Madeleine Carroll, DFJr., Mary Astor, C. Aubrey Smith, Raymond Massey, David Niven.

1938 THE JOY OF LIVING. RKO. April 15. Dir. by Tay Garnett. Irene Dunne, DFJr., Alice Brady, Guy Kibbee,

Jean Dixon, Eric Blore, Billy Gilbert, Franklin Pangborn, Lucille Ball.
THE RAGE OF PARIS. Universal. July 1. Dir. by Henry Koster. DFJr., Danielle Darrieux, Mischa Auer, Helen Broderick, Louis Hayward.
HAVING WONDERFUL TIME. RKO. July 1. Dir. by Alfred Santell. Ginger Rogers, DFJr., Red Skelton, Lucille Ball, Eve Arden, Jack Carson, Donald Meek, Grady Sutton.
THE YOUNG IN HEART. United Artists. Nov. 3. Prod. by Selznick International. Dir. by Richard Wallace. DFJr., Janet Gaynor, Paulette Goddard, Roland Young, Billie Burke, Richard Carlson.

1939 GUNGA DIN. RKO. Feb. 17. Prod. and dir. by George Stevens. Cary Grant, Victor McLaglen, DFJr., Sam Jaffe, Eduardo Cianelli, Joan Fontaine, Robert Coote, Montagu Love.

April 22 Married Mary Lee Epling Hartford in Los Angeles. Three daughters: Daphne (b. 1940), Victoria (b. 1942), Melissa (b. 1947).

THE SUN NEVER SETS. Universal. June 9. Prod. and dir. by Rowland V. Lee. DFJr., Basil Rathbone, Virginia Field, Lionel Atwill, Barbara O'Neil, C. Aubrey Smith.
RULERS OF THE SEA. Paramount. Nov. 17. Prod. and dir. by Frank Lloyd. DFJr., Margaret Lockwood, Will Fyffe, George Bancroft, Montagu Love.

Helped organize The William Allen White Committee (later National Vice-Chairman) and Franco-British War Relief. Headed and personally responsible for Douglas Voluntary Hospitals in U.K. (1939-44).

1940 GREEN HELL. Universal. Jan. 26. Dir. by James Whale. DFJr., Joan Bennett, John Howard, George Sanders, Vincent Price, Alan Hale, George Bancroft.
SAFARI. Paramount. June 14. Dir. by Edward H. Griffith. DFJr., Madeleine Carroll, Tullio Carminati, Muriel Angelus, Lynne Overman, Billy Gilbert.
ANGELS OVER BROADWAY. Columbia. Sept. 30. Prod. by Ben Hecht and DFJr. Dir. by Ben Hecht and Lee Garmes. Written by Ben Hecht. DFJr., Rita Hayworth, Thomas Mitchell, John Qualen, George Watts.

1940-41 Presidential Envoy for Special Mission to South America.

1941 April Commissioned Lieutenant (j.g.) U.S. Naval Reserve. On active duty that summer aboard destroyer on convoy escort in North Atlantic.

THE CORSICAN BROTHERS. Edward Small Productions. Rel. by United Artists, Nov. 28. Dir. by Gregory Ratoff. DFJr., Akim Tamiroff, Ruth Warrick, J. Carroll Naish, H. B. Warner, John Emery, Henry Wilcoxon.

1942 Mine-sweeper patrol and North Atlantic convoy escort duty to Iceland, Scotland, Malta and Murmansk.

1942-44 On planning staff and operations officer for Special Operations, U.S. Amphibious Forces, Atlantic Fleet.

1943 Participated in invasions of Sicily, Italian mainland, Elba and South of France. Later awarded Silver Star (for "conspicuous gallantry," Battle of Salerno), Legion of Merit with "V" for Valor attachment (invasion of South of France); also British D.S.C., French Croix de Guerre with Palm, and Italian War Cross.

1946 Released to Inactive Duty (as Commander; promoted to Captain, 1952).

1946-50 CARE and Share-through-CARE Committee, National Chairman.
Part-time Consultant to Presidential Advisor, Office of the Presidency.

1947 SINBAD THE SAILOR. RKO. March 19. Dir. by Richard Wallace. DFJr., Maureen O'Hara, Anthony Quinn, Walter Slezak, George Tobias, Jane Greer, Mike Mazurki, Sheldon Leonard.
THE EXILE. The Fairbanks Co./Universal-International. Nov. Prod. and written by DFJr. Based on the novel, *His Majesty the King,* by Cosmo Hamilton. Dir. by Max Ophuls. DFJr., Paule Croset, Maria Montez, Nigel Bruce, Henry Daniell, Robert Coote.

1948 THAT LADY IN ERMINE. 20th Century-Fox. Aug. Dir. by Ernst Lubitsch (and Otto Preminger). Betty Grable, DFJr., Cesar Romero, Walter Abel, Reginald Gardiner.

1949 THE FIGHTING O'FLYNN. Fairbanks Co./Universal-International. Feb. Prod. by DFJr. Written by DFJr. and Robert Thoeren. Dir. by Arthur Pierson. DFJr., Helena Carter, Richard Greene, Patricia Medina, Arthur Shields.

March 28 Made honorary Knight Commander, Order of the British Empire, for services to Anglo-American relations.

1950 STATE SECRET (THE GREAT MANHUNT). London Films U.K. rel. April; U.S. rel. Dec. Dir. by Sidney Gilliat. DFJr., Glynis Johns, Jack Hawkins, Herbert Lom.

1951 MISTER DRAKE'S DUCK. Angel Prod. (DFJr. and Daniel Angel). U.K. rel. Jan. Dir. by Val Guest. DFJr., Yolande Donlan, A. E. Matthews, Jon Pertwee, Wilfred Hyde-White.

1952 ANOTHER MAN'S POISON. Angel Prod. (DFJr. and Daniel Angel). U.K. rel. Nov. 1951; U.S. rel. Jan. Dir. by Irving Rapper. Bette Davis, Gary Merrill, Emlyn Williams.

1958 CHASE A CROOKED SHADOW. Associated Dragon. U.K. rel. Jan.; U.S. rel. April. Prod. by DFJr. and Thomas Clyde. Dir. by Michael Anderson. Richard Todd, Anne Baxter, Herbert Lom.

1952-57 Produced 160 one-act plays for television (*Douglas Fairbanks Presents* and *Rheingold Theater*), acting in 40 of them.

1962 *The Shadowed Affair,* television special, with Greer Garson.

1966 Senior Churchill Fellow, Westminster College, Fulton, Missouri.

1968 RED AND BLUE. A.B.C. (Brit.). Part of trilogy written

and directed by Tony Richardson (not released). Vanessa Redgrave, DFJr.
The Canterville Ghost, television special with Sir Michael Redgrave.

1968–69 *My Fair Lady,* special revival in St. Louis, Dallas, and Atlanta; new production in Los Angeles and San Francisco.

1969 Visiting Fellow, St. Cross College, Oxford University.

1970–72 *The Pleasure of His Company,* in Chicago and on tour. (In Toronto in 1974.)

1971 Naval member, U.S. military delegation to SEATO Conference, London.

1972 *Crooked Hearts.* ABC TV. With Rosalind Russell and Maureen O'Sullivan.

1973–74 *The Secretary Bird,* by William Douglas Home, in Chicago and on tour.

1974 Attached for special duties, Joint Chiefs of Staff, Pentagon. Hon. L.L.D., University of Denver. Awarded Italian Order of Merit.

1975 *Present Laughter,* by Noel Coward, in Washington, D.C., and on tour.

PICTURE CREDITS

The authors and editors are grateful to Mary Corliss of the Film Stills Archive of The Museum of Modern Art, New York, for her assistance in acquiring additional stills from the Fairbankses' films. The following photographs are from that archive: page 47 (upper right and center), 53 (upper left), 57, 94 (bottom), 104, 105 (both), 162 (all), 163, 164, 165 (both), 167, 176, 178, 181, 183, 188 (upper right), 191, 192, 194 (bottom). Photographs were also made or supplied by the following photographers and agencies: Acme (AP), 212 (both), 215, 226 (bottom); Anthony Armstrong-Jones, 262, 265 (both); Associated Press, 175, 207, 211, 239 (right), 249 (bottom); Tom Blau, 255, 264, 276; Culver Pictures, 98, 99 (right), 148, 211; Bud Fraser, 237; Martha Holmes, 251; International, 82, 99; *London Daily Express* (Pictorial Parade), 279; London News Agency, 227; Charles Lynch, 215 (top); Cyril Maitland, 273; Raymond Mander and Joe Mitchenson Theatre Collection, 202; Nikolas Muray, 174; *New York Times,* 199 (top); Parish Studios, 182 (center); Planet, 209; Portal Publications, Sausalito, 128; Lloyd S. Pauley, 248; Charles Rhodes, 239 (top); Time-Life Picture Collection, 96 Johnny Florea, 109 Eric Schall, 194 (top), 200, 213, 229-231 George Stroock, 259 Thomas D. MacAvoy; Eileen Tweedy, 62, 205, 245 (lower left), 246 (center), 247 (right); A. V. Swaebe, 270; U.S. Navy, 245 (center); U.S. War Dept.-National Archives, 58; World Wide, 214, 226; *Yorkshire Post,* 278.

Composed in Souvenir Light by DEKR Corporation, Woburn, Massachusetts
Printed by Murray Printing, Forge Village, Massachusetts
Bound by A. Horowitz and Son, Fairfield, New Jersey